CHANGE YOUR MIND TO
CHANGE YOUR REALITY

How Shifting Your Thinking Can Unlock Your Health, Your Relationships, and Your Peace of Mind

KRIS ASHLEY

CHANGE YOUR MIND TO CHANGE YOUR REALITY
How Shifting Your Thinking Can Unlock Your Health,
Your Relationships, and Your Peace of Mind

ISBN Paperback: 978-1-7386416-0-4
ISBN eBook: 978-1-7386416-1-1

Published by: Helping People Press, a wholly owned subsidiary of
The Authority Factory, Toronto, Canada

ENDORSEMENT

"Change Your Mind to Change Your Reality takes you on a voyage of discovery that will break down mental barriers, align your thoughts and desires, and transform your mind at a deeper and more creative level - all to reflect your best and highest good. A must read!"

– Anita Moorjani, New York Times Bestselling Author of Dying to Be Me, What if this is Heaven, and Sensitive is the New Strong

"A refreshing, "must-read" complete guide full of eye-opening insights and heart-opening inspiration. Change Your Mind to Change Your Reality is a total game-changer! A go-to source for personal development, blending scientific and spiritual principles. This book will transform you, how you view the world, and the situations happening in your life. I recommend it to anyone who wishes to learn effective strategies for self-improvement."

– Victoria M. Gallagher, Author of Practical Law of Attraction and How to Manifest Your Soulmate

"Kris is an author who empowers people! She gives clear guidance and wisdom on how to create the life you want through understanding how your energy works in the world and providing plentiful stories, examples and strategies. I highly recommend!"

– Melanie A Dean, PhD, Author and winner of three book awards for The Hidden Power of Emotions

"Cheers to Kris for her passion on this topic, and for how deeply she goes in service to her audience. Her chapter and perspective on forgiveness alone is worth the price of admission, and I invite readers to take the knowledge and encouragement provided in this book to heart. There's a lot of gold here."

— *Andrew Kap, Author of The Last Law of Attraction Book You'll Ever Need To Read*

"I don't know how it can get more practical than this! Kris Ashley really gets it when it comes to manifesting. And while it's fun to think about all the metaphysical aspects or "woo woo" aspects of it, when you really want to see results, there are certain things you absolutely must do to have all that actually work, and experience true transformation. Kris lays out all the steps for you, and even addresses what to do if you're not seeing the change you want. If you do what she says, you cannot fail. It's simple science."

— *Bob Doyle, featured Expert in The Secret MeetBobDoyle.com*

"A very enjoyable read. Kris delves into just the right balance of human psychology + mindset practice, and pairs it with her own experience and know-how to give you a set of solutions to truly change your life. She knows what most people don't, that our thoughts cause our behaviors, and those in turn create our realities, for better or worse. She shows you how to turn it positive in any situation and end up with what she deems your dream life. I got a lot out of this actionable book. Highly recommended."

— *Nick Trenton, Author of Stop Overthinking: 23 Techniques to Relieve Stress, Stop Negative Spirals, Declutter Your Mind, and Focus on the Present*

"I was honored to read Kris Ashley's amazing book. This is a groundbreaking book on reality creation. Kris has a unique writing style that is quite personal and describes complicated concepts in an entertaining manner. This is a guidebook for creating your dream life. Kris outlines a number of concepts that will help you to shift your thinking and belief system to create the life that you want."

— *Brian Scott, Author of The Reality Revolution: The Mind-Blowing Movement to Hack Your Reality*

"Highly recommend! Kris does a fantastic job of giving us the most valuable tools to navigate this life with."

— *Sarah Breskman Cosme, Author of A Hypnotist's Journey to Atlantis*

"Being able to deliberately attract anything starts with YOU being deliberate – about what you think, say, do, observe, or give your attention to. Kris provides tools you can use at home with your family or at work building your business with the right mind-set. In her book Change Your Mind to Change Your Reality, she provides tools for applying mind-set approaches, applying the Law of Attraction deliberately, and more. The Law of Attraction is always responding to what you are giving your attention to… let this book help send the right message and vibes."

— *Michael J Losier, Canadian Author of Law of Attraction – The Science of Attracting More of What You Want and Less of What You Don't*

"Change Your Mind to Change Your Reality, outlines multiple methods that can support you along your spiritual journey while navigating the chaos that can be everyday life. The concepts are written in easy to understand language which allows a deeper shift to occur. This book encourages you to think different and change your mind to see changes in your life."

— *Latha Jay, Spiritual Manifestation Coach and Bestselling Author of The Law of Attraction, Manifestation Journal*

For Mom.

Contents

INTRODUCTION

   Imagine that you are the picture of health, love, joy, and happiness. You have a special someone in your life who is compassionate and loving and the perfect match for you. You are passionate about your work and have a paycheck that makes you feel comfortable and secure. You're hitting all the personal and professional milestones important to you. You laugh a lot. You are surrounded by people who cheer you on, love you, and truly want the best for you. You have free time and enough money so you can pursue any hobby that sparks your soul. You hold no grudges against anyone, and you've released any emotions or limiting beliefs that were holding you back. You are at peace. You love your reflection in the mirror and feel confident in your own skin. Any time a challenge comes your way, you know exactly what to do to handle it with grace and ease and spin it into something positive that ends up helping you out in the long run. When you look out at the world, you see fairness, harmony, and beauty. Life is *good*!

Does this sound like a description of your life right now? If it does, that's amazing and I am so happy for you. If it does not, does it sound like something you want? How about does it sound like something you think you *could* have? Is there a little voice in the back of your head right now, telling you, *That's impossible, no one can attain all of that*, or *at least not me*? Maybe your mind immediately jumps to all of the ways you are lacking, not worthy, or even suffering.

If it doesn't sound like your current life or if you're thinking any of these thoughts, don't worry—you're not alone. Three out of four people report feeling lonely and disconnected, like they are just going through the motions in life and that it's happening to them and they are not in control. These people report feeling powerless, stressed out, insecure, anxious, lonely, and/or depressed. And they look at others whom life seems to come with ease to and wonder how it is that they seem to get everything they want. Some feel like they're stuck in a rut while others resolve to the fact that their life is just average and lacks the potential and/or opportunity to be extraordinary. Another 60 percent say they are dissatisfied with their work. I could go on and on, but the most interesting statistic of all to me is that psychologists estimate 70 to 90 percent of people's thoughts are negative and repetitive. This book is about making the correlation between your thoughts and your current reality and teaching you how to make a shift.

For those of us who have gone through a spiritual awakening, we often describe it as a defining moment in our life. It's like a line drawn vertically across our time line, clearly delineating two separate sides: who we were before the awakening and who we became after. For me that moment happened in 2002. I was seventeen, and a boy I was dating handed me a book called *The Ancient Secret of the Flower of Life* that blew my mind wide open and awoke in me an intense, insatiable hunger for even more knowledge. I couldn't get enough. My life became one big quest to learn, grow, heal, and expand every aspect of myself, a purpose that drove me onward.

I've collected so much knowledge from such a wide variety of sources in the twenty years since that awakening. The knowledge was seemingly unrelated, yet as I kept diving deep, patterns began to emerge and I started to realize it was all connected. Right now we are experiencing the biggest awakening humanity has had in recent history. The wave has been pulling back, rapidly moving toward an ever quickly forming swell, and each day that swell reaches greater and greater heights. Soon it will crash over, and humanity will be thrust forward in our evolution.

And so I compiled this book of everything I've learned, of the teachers I've studied who lit the pathway. It is the culmination of two decades of study and practice. I give you a shortcut to what took me twenty years to learn, so that you can live your dream life now and enjoy all the pleasure and joy that come with it. You can view it as classroom notes for this experience we call life.

This book is my gift to the world, and I have poured my whole heart into it. There are lots of books out there on the Law of Attraction, healing, forgiveness, and how your thoughts influence your life, and you will find I've referenced many throughout this book as well. But this book is different because I synthesize material from various teachings and take you so far beyond these concepts. I show you how to change your mind in every corner of your life and ask you to consider possibilities that may seem foreign to you at first.

My hope is to empower everyone who picks up this book. I want you to be able to turn the final page feeling energized and confident. I want your mind to be expanded and the way in which you view the world forever changed. I want you to know that you are in control of what happens in your life and your lens alone dictates your reaction and how you perceive it. I want you to let go of grudges, find meaning and purpose, and get everything your heart desires, whether it be that perfect relationship, the promotion you've been wanting, the healing you've been working toward, or the courage to follow your dreams. I want you to find ways to show yourself love and take care of yourself, so you can then be the best version of yourself for yourself and your friends, family, community, and the world. I want you to understand that you are more than a body, you are more than a mind, and what you see through your eyes when you look out into the world isn't the whole picture. I want you to see the beauty around you, everywhere, and know that it is radiating directly from you.

And the best part is that I'm not going to do any of these things for you—*you* have the power inside of you to do them all. It all comes from you. I just offer you a road map. So come discover how a simple change in perspective can completely change the life you are living.

And so our journey together begins…

CHAPTER 1

WHY CHANGE YOUR MIND?

I'm going to start off by making a radical statement and then spend the rest of this book expanding on it for you.

The beliefs you have about yourself and
the world, and the thoughts that you think,
create the reality you live in. They quite literally
shape the world you see around you, including
the circumstances you find yourself in, the
relationships you have with other people, your
health, your success, and so much more. And
by changing your mind and adopting a new
set of beliefs and thoughts, you can completely
transform all these circumstances and the world
at large around you.

This has proven true time and time again throughout my life, and I believe it so deeply in my core. But I didn't used to think this way. I was an incredibly shy and insecure kid. I was super scrawny and got made fun of for my body. This impacted me so

1

much that I didn't wear shorts for the better part of a decade. I had crippling social anxiety, but I was also angry at the world. When I was twelve years old, I went through trauma that severely impacted my life for a great many years. After surviving four years of sexual abuse at the hands of a family member, that truth got out to my large extended family, and what was once a tight-knit family that did everything together, even sang any time we were around each other, split down the middle. Family members whom I had previously been close with told me they no longer loved me and I wasn't their family anymore. I was no longer permitted to see two of my cousins who had been my best friends. One day we were inseparable, and the next day they were like ghosts. I have no idea what they were told about what happened. I was left with PTSD, a horrible self-image, lots of negative emotions like guilt and anger that I didn't know how to cope with, and self-harming behaviors. I turned to drugs. I turned to cutting. I turned to anything to numb the pain.

My life changed dramatically at age seventeen when I was handed a book that completely changed how I thought about the world. It changed my way of thinking, my way of being, my way of understanding and moving through life. As I turned the pages, it hit me so hard that what was written inside it felt like the truth, and like a sleeper agent, something inside of me woke up. When I finished it, I started reaching for more. I became insatiable. I started devouring every metaphysical, spiritual, new age, and personal development book I could get my hands on. I watched documentaries. I attended seminars, workshops, and retreats. I dove in headfirst to all of the teachings I could find. I became obsessed with metaphysics, quantum physics, reincarnation, meditation, yoga, the Law of Attraction, the ancient astronaut theory, sacred geometry, biohacking, functional medicine, and different healing modalities. I couldn't get enough. Every book was like a new door opening in an unending hallway. I wanted more. I needed more. I was hooked. My life became one big quest to learn, grow, heal, and expand every aspect of myself. It became my life's mission, a purpose that drove me onward.

As I began to change my mind and get better, my mother began to get worse. Her family had been ripped down the seams. She started to get physically sick, with both serious illnesses and with strange afflictions we had never even heard of before and doctors could barely explain. She slept. A lot. At the height of it, she was on a Fentanyl patch, taking about eleven different pills every day, and sleeping for all but a few hours of daylight. She fell down all the time. She nodded off at the dinner table. She forgot conversations we'd had the day prior. This lasted over ten years while I lived with unbelievable guilt that I had destroyed my family and broken my mother.

In the end, it was my mother who inadvertently became my biggest teacher. For every step she took deeper into depression and illness, I climbed hand over hand in the other direction, out of the proverbial tunnel. I saw firsthand what happens to a human body and spirit when they go down that path. And then I saw what happened to my own body and spirit as I decided to change my mind about the nature of reality. I made a promise to myself that I would do everything I could to heal physically, mentally, emotionally, and spiritually, and that I would always prioritize my health.

My mother's story isn't unique. So many people have accepted that illness is our natural state and wellness is difficult to achieve. They allow their thoughts and emotions to take wild control over their life. They have fed into the idea that as you get older, you start to feel worse, and taking prescription medication is the only chance you have at some reprieve. If you're lucky, you have some good moments in between, but suffering is inevitable. They don't take the time to heal emotionally, to listen to their body, and to question why they're sick in the first place. Growth and learning are not priorities for them. It's almost as if they've given up, settled, and just accepted whatever life throws their way.

Learning and growth should never be over. I love finding stuff that blows my mind wide open and sends my thoughts expanding into directions they never before knew existed. I love trying out new exercises, healing modalities, and programs to improve even further.

People look at me now and think I've got it made and things come easy to me. That is because I've crafted my dream life—the best husband I could possibly ask for, a beautiful dream house we designed together, a job I love where I feel like I'm living my life's purpose and following my passions, free time to enjoy doing what I love, and the paycheck I've always wanted. I am confident in my body and in who I am, and I love my life. I don't have a shred of doubt in my abilities and talents. But perhaps most importantly, I move confidently through life knowing that I can design the life I want and anything life throws my way I am fully capable of not only handling but spinning to work in my favor so that I may level up even more. I view life as something fun and exciting I get to participate in and don't take it overly seriously. And I now am a life coach, helping others to achieve what I have, which is so incredibly rewarding.

I share my story not to brag but in the hopes that other people can be inspired and see a possibility to rise out of their own ashes, to shift their mindset, and to know they don't have to be their past.

I'm not asking you to change your mind about religion. This book does not associate with any religion, nor do I want to ask you to change your opinion on religion. That's something sacred and personal to you. Whatever you believe in on that matter can still fit nicely with this new information. This is a book for everyone having a human experience, because that is what we're all sharing right now.

Are Your Current Beliefs Helping or Hindering You?

Have you ever had the experience of someone from a younger generation asking you what something is? One of my cousin's children once asked me what a floppy disk was when we were cleaning out a room in my aunt's house and found one. She thought it was a toy replica of the save icon on her computer. Now we might laugh at this because we have the experience of it being a floppy disk and know the save icon was modeled after the floppy disk, but imagine if she were in the room alone and saw that object. She would say "That's a toy" based on the fact that to her, it was a 3D object of something she's seen in 2D. If *you* were alone in the room with it, you'd say, "That's a floppy disk." What about civilizations who have never even seen a computer before? What might they think it is, other than a toy or a disk? So the question then is: what is the object? Is it a floppy disk or is it a toy, or is it something else? The answer is: it's none of the above. The point is that the object itself isn't anything. You place meaning on top of it when you look at it, interact with it, and label it. Your past experiences with the object dictate your understanding of it today. All objects, situations, circumstances, things that happen to you, things that people say to you, and so on are all neutral. You assign meaning to them based on your own experience.

Information is neutral, but your response is not. The way you process that information is not. Everything you've gone through in your past—the beliefs of adults you grew up around, cultural conditioning, inherent biases, the kids who made fun of you on the playground, the boss who said you're not good enough, your crush who rejected you, your mindset and emotions, etcetera—all helps build your belief system that serves as the lens through which you view life. Ten different people could witness the same situation and see it from ten different points of view, all adamantly insisting that their way is the right way.

Our lens tells us that the world is either a scary place or a loving place, that people are to be trusted or we should always be on the defense, that we have lots of opportunities or we are gridlocked into place. And this lens starts to create experiences and circumstances for us in our outer world. Our inner world creates our outer world. If we think and believe from a place of ease, comfort, safety, love, confidence, and abundance, then that is what we will experience in our life. If we experience thoughts, beliefs, and feelings of struggle, unhappiness, pain, anger, resentment, guilt, insecurities, and fear, then those will be what we experience. The very things we don't want to happen, will happen.

Unfortunately, in modern society, so many people wallow in fear, doubt, worry, insecurities, envy, anger, mistrust, and things they don't want to happen. We've been taught that thinking these types of thoughts is normal and something we can't control, but we've been taught the wrong lesson. True change can only come after unlearning all of those lessons and undoing that conditioning, so we can instead gain the awareness, support, and empowerment to live our best life. What we focus on most becomes our reality.

The biggest obstacle holding most people back from living the life of their dreams is themselves. Negative thoughts, habits, emotions, and beliefs hold us back from seeing new possibilities and solutions and from taking steps toward our dreams, because they give us a narrow view of the world around us. They keep us sick if we are ill, lonely if we are lacking love in our lives, holding onto resentments rather than finding connection. We need to shift our thinking—change our minds—in order to see all the possibilities expand out before us. Only then will we realize how much better life can be.

This is not to say you can't experience fear, doubt, worry, envy, stress, and insecurities from time to time. We're human beings, and these emotions are part of our experience. Everyone experiences them, even highly successful people. The difference is that some people know how to use these feelings to their advantage, how to let go of them, and how to reframe their thinking around them.

When you look up the word "belief" in the thesaurus, one of the antonyms for it is "truth." This might seem strange at first glance, but if you think about it, your beliefs are mostly based on your opinions or the opinions others have taught you. Opinions are not founded in truth, so you could even go so far as to say that your beliefs are lies you tell yourself and others tell you. We base our lives around these lies, oftentimes to our own detriment and suffering.

At their worst, our beliefs create judgments of the way others live their life, create the notion of people being *others* or separate from us, make us hold onto bitter anger and resentment toward others, and even start wars. We tend to have this notion that our beliefs and the thoughts that go along with them are steadfast. Most of us stand unwavering in our beliefs. Our way is correct, and everyone else's way is wrong. You only need to look at any two opposing groups of people in the world to see proof of this. We build the story of who we are around our beliefs, and the idea of changing our beliefs seems to fundamentally take away our identity. The question to really ask yourself, though, is are your beliefs allowing your life to expand or contract? Are they lifting you up or bringing you down?

When we are rigid in our beliefs, we only see the world from a narrow viewpoint and then only have a narrow amount of opportunities and possibilities available.

Now that you understand better just how incredibly powerful our belief system is, how that lens creates our reality independent of what we may want our reality to be, let's explore if it's really possible to make this kind of monumental change.

Can Your Belief System Really Be Changed?

We change our minds all the time, like about what outfit we want to wear, what we want to eat for dinner, and what movie we want to watch. Yet for the "big things," we seem firmly rooted in our beliefs. This inflexibility can keep us stuck, unable to see things past our limited viewpoint and incapable of shifting our perspective and finding new solutions. The idea of changing your mind threatens to shake your foundations to the core, and though this is a positive thing necessary to change your reality, you may perceive change as a threat and fear it like many people do. So if you're meeting with some resistance from yourself, know that this is a perfectly normal response. The truth, though, is that this perceived threat and fear is a projection of ego, which I'll expand on later on.

Once you change your beliefs and thoughts, you'll be pleasantly surprised to find that it is without catastrophe raining down. You won't lose your sense of self. With this fresh new field of vision, entire worlds of possibility you never conceived of will open up before you. It's like suddenly having the key to a new, magical land you never knew existed. All you have to do is turn the lock and open the door and your world can completely transform.

At the end of the day, you get to decide what's real. Everything is only as real as you believe it is. You are not a slave to your circumstances. In fact, you can redefine and reinvent yourself as many times as you'd like.

You have the power to change your mind at any point in time. You can peel off the layers of perceptions that do not serve you, the stories that you've built around yourself, the opinions that others have laid on top of you, and get back down to your core being. Wouldn't it be amazing to get back down to your real self, the carefree, joyful, completely worthy state you felt as a child? That's who you really are, and feeling that way is your birthright! And if you're able to change your mind about who you really are, then it will send ripple effects through every area of your life and make changing your mind about the rest much easier.

If you want to change your current life situation, you have to learn to change your mind. This is true for everything from your mood, to your health, to success in your career, to your relationships.

The most successful people in the world invest in their own growth, their own development. They are students of life, constantly seeking new knowledge so that they can continue to expand in all areas. They are constantly testing and moving the fence line of their comfort zone and playing with their edges often, because they know that's where growth happens. They try new things, are open to new ideas, talk to people with different points of view, expose themselves to things that shock their senses, and summon up courage to do things that scare them. They explore and surround themselves with people who know more about various topics than they do so they can constantly learn in the areas where they are weaker. And because of all of this learning and new experiences, they allow their beliefs to be more liquid and less firm, less cemented. They are flexible and allow their minds to remain open.

So, here's your first opportunity to shift your thinking. I'm going to ask you to be open to the possibility that the way you see things isn't the only way. I'm going to ask you to suspend your disbelief and come on a ride with me. Take what I'm saying at face value, even if you have to pretend. You could simply pretend I am going to tell you a wonderful fairytale. But do the exercises and put these teachings into practice in your life. I guarantee that if you follow the exercises, practices, and advice in this book, you'll find that your life will completely and totally change. New possibilities will open up before you, you'll feel better, your outlook on life will shift, and you'll move through the world with more confidence and ease. Just open a tiny piece of your mind up to the consideration that maybe all of this is true.

CHAPTER 2

UNDERSTANDING YOUR
DIVINE NATURE

We tend to think the world around us, what we experience through our five senses, is all there is. Across the variety of beliefs in our society about a higher power, higher intelligence, or that there is or is not more to life than we know, if you listen in on any passing conversation, you usually find that it revolves around very "earthly" topics such as our jobs, the TV show we're binge-watching, deciphering text messages from our crush, the most recent appalling news story, the latest trend on social media, the newest celebrity couple, gossip about our neighbors, and family drama. It's rare to overhear a conversation about the meaning of life, death, aliens, spirituality, unconditional love, other dimensions, ancient archaeology, wisdom teachings, or anything else with more depth than that which we find in our day-to-day lives. Our conversations mirror our thoughts, and our thoughts are so often consumed by similar things: how many likes we're getting on social media, our illnesses, the things we feel guilty about, our bank account, the people we feel envious of or angry at, our leaky roof that needs tending to, all of the emails that are piling up in our inbox, all of the irritating people we have to deal with as we run our errands, and so on. So many people are stuck in the daily grind of work, money, entertainment, sleep, that they've come to believe this equals life as a human being. They seldom pause to ask the bigger questions.

What if everything you believed so strongly *wasn't* true?

Allow me to offer you a different perspective about the reality around you. Earth isn't a place we are just born into to live a rat race and then die. It's not a meaningless existence. And it's not our only shot.

There is so much more to this "reality" than meets the eye—literally and figuratively. The human eye can only see 0.0035 percent of the light spectrum. That means we are unable to see over 99 percent of what is going on around us. Most of our existence is invisible to us and the majority of the world is hidden from us in plain sight. We get clues to how the rest of this existence works, though. For example, quantum physics shows us how observing something makes it behave differently. Reality is constantly morphing before our very own eyes.

There's a famous experiment in quantum physics called the "Double-Slit Experiment," where a machine sends something such as a single photon or electron through a piece of board that has a slit in it and a pattern emerges on the wall behind the board when that photon or electron reaches it. If the thing travels as a particle, it shows one pattern on the wall behind it. If it travels as a wave, it shows another. When there was only one slit in the board, the electron showed a particle pattern on the wall behind the machine. This matches what we believe about the world, that matter is made up of particles. But when there were two slits in the board, it showed a wave pattern on the wall behind the machine. To have a wave pattern insinuates that it went through both slits simultaneously and the two "pieces" somehow interfered with each other, which is impossible according to the way we understand the world.

Well, it gets even weirder. The scientists conducting the experiment decided there was no way an electron—*matter!*—could be traveling through both slits simultaneously, so they set up a detector to observe the experiment to figure out what was going on. But when the detector was set up, the electron traveled through one of the two slits only, and only a particle pattern emerged on the back wall. So the electron went from being a wave back to a particle. The only difference between the two versions was that the experiment was being witnessed by the detector. The electron acted differently, as though it knew it was being watched. No matter what the scientists did, as long as they were observing the experiment, they only got a particle pattern, but as soon as they ran the experiment again without observing it, the wave pattern returned. This happened whether they used electrons, photons of light, or molecules. The experiment teaches us that electrons are waves, but when we look at them and measure them, they appear like particles to us. It also suggests that through observation, consciousness is actively creating.

Other scientists took it a step further and created the "Delayed-Choice Experiment" to try to capture this logic-defying behavior once and for all. This experiment was conducted with photons of light. They placed a special crystal at the slit that would split a photon into a pair of identical photons and, once they passed through it, would travel off into different directions. One photon would go toward the back wall while the other photon would go toward the detector.

To their awe, when they tried it with the detector in the room, it still showed a particle pattern on the back wall. When they removed the detector, a wave pattern emerged once again. They then tried to move the detector back a bit so that the first photon would reach the wall *before* the second photon would reach the detector. They were confident this would produce the wave pattern because *information can't travel backward through time*. When they ran the experiment, they *still* couldn't get the wave pattern to return. Even when the second photon was detected by the detector *after* the first photon hit the wall, it *still* showed a particle pattern. This means that through the act of observing, events that had *already happened* were changed.

So the questions really become: Why does observing something make it change? Is there more to all forms of matter, including us, than what there appears to be at first glance? Is every single person creating what they see?

Everything in our universe is made of atoms. If you think back to science class from when you were in school, you might believe an atom has a physical structure. Quantum physicists, however, realized atoms are made up of vortices of energy that are constantly spinning and vibrating, and each "tangible thing" in our world that is made up of atoms radiates a unique energy signature. Have you ever seen the wind lift up some leaves and make them spin, like a mini tornado? To imagine an atom, think of that spinning funnel but take away the leaves. What you have left is a spinning vortex of invisible energy.

In *The Biology of Belief*, cell biologist Bruce Lipton explains what an atom would look like if it were possible to view it with a microscope. He explains that from far away it would look only like a blurry sphere. The closer you go to it, the less in focus it would become. And finally, as you reached it, it would completely disappear and you would see nothing—only a physical void would remain. This is because the atom isn't solid. It's invisible energy that is vibrating and spinning, not something tangible that you can see. The conclusion that we can then make? Everything is energy in our universe and matter itself is an illusion.

Quantum physics to ancient texts from various civilizations all report similar findings supporting that reality is an illusion and we are constantly projecting out into the world that which is in our mind. You are so much more powerful than you know, and Earth and life as a human is so different than what you may perceive.

Do you ever wonder why you're here? What it's all for? What your purpose is? What happens next?

What if we are not human beings having a spiritual experience but spiritual beings having a human experience? We have the power to call into our lives anything that we would like to have, and we live in an intelligent universe that responds to our power by manifesting whatever it is we claim. We do this by the thoughts we think, which impact the emotions we feel and the vibrations we put out. Everything is energy, after all.

Thoughts Create Things

The Law of Attraction is a universal law that says you will attract into your life whatever you focus on. When you focus your energy and attention on what you want rather than what you don't want, you will attract that thing to you. There are ways we can amplify it, such as pretending as though we already have it, feeling the emotion of having it, and feeling grateful for having it already. It's like fake it till you make it.

The reason this works is that we have to match the frequency of the thing we want. It's like changing the channel on a TV. If you're watching the History channel and want to watch *Animal Planet*, no matter how many times you hope for *Animal Planet*, you're still going to have the History channel until you actually pick up the remote and change the channel. We can't create our new life if we're working at the same frequency of the life we have now.

Your thoughts create your reality. Your current life—your relationships, job, health, everything—is a direct reflection of your current thoughts, the way you feel about yourself and the world, and your belief structure. What you see appearing in your life is the universe's way of mirroring your thoughts, emotions, and frequency back to you.

And if this is a little hard to understand, then think about this: Everything you see around you was once a thought—the chair you're sitting on, the clothing you're wearing, the computer you're using, the buildings you walk past every day. All of these things were once in someone's imagination before they were "real" and tangible. If you think about the world, everything in it was first created as a thought, then turned into a tangible thing. Our imagination and our thoughts create the blueprints for things first, before those things manifest in the real world. In fact, that is why humans have imaginations. Our imagination is our tool for envisioning all that we desire. If you can dream it up, it can become real.

There's a story about the day EPCOT first opened at Disney World. It was a huge success the first day, with crowds and crowds of people and everyone was happy. A reporter walked up to Roy Disney, Walt's brother, and asked him, "This must be a bittersweet day for you, huh?"

Roy was confused and asked the reporter what he meant because it was obviously an amazing day.

The reporter said, "Well, EPCOT is open and doing great, but you must be sad because Walt isn't here to see it."

Roy looked at him and responded, "Walt was a visionary. Trust me, Walt saw all of this."

Now what he meant by Walt being a visionary was that he saw it all in his mind before sketching out the ideas and putting pen to paper. He created EPCOT first in his mind, in his imagination, before it ever became a reality. He used the Law of Attraction.

Once you understand this principle, I promise you you'll only ever use your thoughts as tools. And once you truly learn how to master this power—because that's what it is, a power—life becomes a game. It's fun! You get to call into your life whatever you'd like. You can view your life like a video game, where you can assemble and build everything you want from optimal health, a dream career, the partner you want, to the time and money to be able to do whatever you'd like—everything and anything you can imagine.

Outside circumstances such as receiving a big paycheck, stepping outside to a beautiful sunny day, and being in a loving relationship don't bring you happiness. *You* bring you happiness by deciding that you want to be happy with the thoughts you think. And you can change your mind about whether to be sad or to be happy in an instant. You deserve all of the happiness in the world, and you can have it. You just have to know how to claim it. You just have to start to turn on your power and recognize that you are the designer of your own life. Because the truth is, our natural state is one of love, joy, peace, health, and wellness. Pain and illness are the anomaly, and they are signals that something is out of alignment. And as you begin to relinquish your small, negative, and constricting thoughts about yourself and the world around you and instead step into your true power, abundance will start to flow into your life where there was once lack.

Your life could look completely different mere weeks from now. This concept may sound far-fetched, but it works. And I'm not going to be the one to prove it to you over the course of this book. You're going to prove it to yourself. But first, a story…

In 2010, I was living in San Francisco, California and had just gotten out of a four-year relationship. I had moved out to the Bay Area with my now ex-boyfriend a year and a half earlier and still didn't know many people in the city. I was going to be starting grad school in a few months and was only working part-time at a retail store selling tie-dye T-shirts on the famous corner of Haight and Ashbury. I decided to make a list of everything I wanted in a "dream guy." It included all of the big things from honesty and loyalty, to having the same sense of humor as me, enjoying the same music and hobbies, a love of animals, and so on, and I read it morning, noon, and night. Anytime I would think of a new quality, I would add it to my list. The list was in the notes app on my cell phone, so it was always with me.

Two weeks later, I was bored and lonely and decided to sign on to Match.com. I honestly can't tell you what possessed me to do that. I had never thought about online dating before that moment. Not once had it crossed my mind or sounded appealing when heard about it in passing conversations. It was almost as if the action I was taking wasn't my own. At the time, Match had you fill out a profile and then would tease you with your top five matches before they made you pay for their service. You could see one photo of each match and a short blip about them, which was maybe a paragraph or two. My top match on there was a cute guy named Shane. I thought, *If there's guys like this on there, I guess I'll pay the thirty bucks.* I paid the fee, messaged him, and we talked every day for two weeks. He was the only person I talked to on there. We finally had our first date two weeks later, and he turned out to be every single thing on my list. Twelve years later, we are still together and happily married. I told two of my other friends my tactic, and they both tried it out. They made lists of all of the qualities of the man of their dreams, and both met their future husbands soon after.

Earth is a School

One of the most influential people in changing my mind about why we're here and what our purpose is was a woman named Dolores Cannon. She was a famous hypnotist who one day accidentally regressed a patient into a past life. She then spent decades regressing patients into past lives and wrote nineteen books chronicling her sessions. Her books are literally the transcribed recordings of her sessions, and they're fascinating. They'll blow your mind wide open. For the first decade or so when she regressed people, they went back into lives on Earth. But slowly, the regressed patients ended up beyond our earthly plane and started describing incredible things about the universe. What I find so fascinating about her work are two things:

1. Much of what her patients said under hypnosis was corroborated by other spiritual teachings I have read.

2. She regressed hundreds of thousands of people from all over the world, with completely different backgrounds and beliefs, who didn't know each other, yet in this deep-trance state, they all reported similar things.

She developed her own hypnosis technique, which she called QHHT (Quantum Healing Hypnosis Technique). I myself have gotten two QHHT sessions, and both of them were incredibly healing and completely changed my life.

Now I know some people will read this and think it's total BS. So I want to share a story about what happened because of my session that had nothing to do with a past life and everything to do with a medical condition in my body I knew nothing about until I talked about it while under hypnosis.

The first half of each QHHT session is spent exploring two different past lives, and during the second half, the patient's personality is asked to recede and what Dolores called their subconscious is asked to come to the forefront. I like to think of it more as their Higher Self. Whatever it is, it's an all-knowing force and the practitioner can ask it things the person would have no way of knowing about. Most people get QHHT sessions for insights from this higher intelligence such as why they're going through something major in their life, like an illness. With the knowledge comes understanding and true healing. There are a multitude of accounts both from Dolores and the flourishing QHHT community of immediate and permanent healings that have taken place during sessions.

During my second session, we did a body scan at the end, which in a QHHT session is when the practitioner asks your subconscious to scan your body to see if you have any diseases or injuries you aren't consciously aware of. A lump in my left breast was found, but I was told that I didn't need to worry, it would resolve itself on its own as long as I stopped getting caught up in earthly drama and emotions. As I was talking about it under hypnosis, I felt some energy right at the top of my left breast. After the session, I couldn't wait to tell my husband about the past lives I had explored and all of the amazing information I had gotten. I spent a long time telling him all of the details and then kind of glazed over the part about the lump on my breast. I wasn't worried since I had been told it would resolve itself and be okay.

He wasn't so convinced. "That's not the kind of thing you mess around with," Shane adamantly responded. "Early detection is everything with that kind of stuff. You should go get it checked out."

To appease him but not really expecting anything, I made an appointment with the women's health services at my local hospital for a breast exam. When the doctor got to my left breast and felt the part where I had felt energy, her face scrunched up. "I don't feel a lump," she started slowly, "but the tissue here feels different. It feels harder, kind of crinkly even. I'm going to send you upstairs to get a mammogram."

"Right now?" I asked in shock. This was becoming very real.

She typed something into the computer. "Yep, it's already ordered. I'd rather err on the side of caution. The second part of the test will be an ultrasound, and someone will call you to make an appointment for that next week. Go up right now."

I texted Shane in shock as I waited for the elevator, and he responded, "Are you okay? Do you need to talk?" I didn't have time to answer though, because I found myself standing in front of the check-in counter. I told the woman my doctor had felt some weird tissue and sent me right up.

"They stopped doing mammograms at four today," the woman said, sounding more disappointed than I was. It was 4:15 pm. Then she said, "Let me just run back and see if they're still here." She disappeared around the corner and ran back a minute later, saying triumphantly, "They're here and they're going to take you!" She pushed a clipboard and pen into my hands. "Here, fill this out really quick."

The mammogram findings seemed to come back normal, though my breast tissue was "dense" so they couldn't find anything. Shane and I sighed some relief.

A week later, I found myself at the ultrasound clinic. I could see a dark spot on the screen that the technician measured, and my heart started pounding. When the doctor came in, she explained that I had fiber-cystic tissue growing in that exact spot and it had

CHANGE YOUR MIND TO CHANGE YOUR REALITY

grown together to form a mass. She reassured me that the mass was benign and there was nothing to worry about.

What a trip!

I texted Shane on my way to the parking lot, and his response back was, "Whoa, that's insane that what your subconscious said was true. If that part's true, then all of it has to be true!"

It certainly solidified the validity of the more "out-there" concepts in my mind.

Hypnosis subjects who regressed to the place between lifetimes reported that Earth is a school. And it's one of many schools. And you are not a human being at all but a soul pretending to be a human being for a short period of time. What is this Earth school all about? The main lesson we are meant to learn here on this earthly plane is how to manipulate energy—how to use the Law of Attraction. We all have the power within us to manifest anything we'd like, but as with anything we *can* do, we must learn *how* to do it, just like we were born with the ability to read but had to learn how to use that power in order to decipher written words.

As we move up in levels of consciousness through our next reincarnations, into higher dimensions, this power will become even more automatic. We'll think something, and it will immediately appear before us. This is why time exists in our 3D earthly experience – so that we have a buffer between what we manifest and that thing materializing in our life. This buffer doesn't exist in higher dimensions so it's important to master this here now. Because you don't want to manifest something negative and have it appear immediately into your life. So we're learning here now, in this lifetime, where it takes longer for the thing we're manifesting to show up. It's part of the homework that helps us learn.

Cultures from all over the world believe in this power for us to manifest, to attract into our lives that which we desire. Gregg Braden wrote an incredible book called *The Isaiah Effect: Decoding the Lost Science of Prayer and Prophecy* about the Isaiah Scroll, one of the best preserved and the only fully intact scroll from the Dead Sea Scrolls. The ancient Essenes who'd created the scrolls wrote about this same power to call into our life that which we want and how we are all connected to each other and the earth. Some people call it prayer, some call it manifesting, some call it the Law of Attraction. But the concept itself is ancient knowledge, no matter the name given to it.

My brother-in-law has a close relationship with Buddhist monks who live at a monastery in the Himalayas. A few years back, some of the monks were going to be visiting and doing some work in California where we all live and needed a place to stay. My in-laws offered their vacation house in Lake Tahoe for them and then met the monks there to make sure they got settled in, knew where everything was, and had everything they needed. At the end of the day, the monks asked both of my in-laws what was something they each wished for because they would pray on it for them as a way to thank them for their kindness and hospitality. My father-in-law was approaching retirement age and said he wanted to sell his business. He owned a metal forging company with his two brothers. It was a very niched and antiquated business, with plenty of challenges because it wasn't super energy efficient and China did the same thing for much cheaper, so they were losing customers. To top it all off, the family dynamics involved complicated things. He couldn't imagine selling it with ease. The monks said they would pray on it, and my father-in-law graciously thanked them.

While this thought of selling was always in the back of his mind, the meeting with the monks brought it more into the forefront. He spoke the words out loud, named them, cast his spell out into the universe. One month later, a company he had never heard of approached him out of the blue and asked if he was interested in selling. They ended up doing the deal, and he's now retired.

When we incarnate into our human bodies, we forget our true spiritual nature. An illusion comes down over our eyes like a curtain, hiding behind it all that is truly real. It wouldn't be a true learning experience if we remembered what we were supposed to learn, after all. So the reality that you see outside of yourself is part of the illusion. It's like we've been dropped into a video game world. It can be anything you want but collectively, humanity has come up with what you see around you. Everything we see outside of ourselves in this lifetime is part of this illusion, this school. We learn the perceived "rules" of the school—aka the programming of our beliefs about what is "real"—from a very young age. We learn about religion, morals, traditional education, the government, the importance of working, money, punishment, war, politics, beauty standards, laws, science, status, and class. We learn from our parents, our teachers, our lawmakers, our employers, the television. By the time we are adults, we are so indoctrinated into this story of reality that we don't question anything. The illusion becomes our comfort zone and all we know is conformity.

The truth according to Dolores Cannon's hypnosis subjects is that we all come from the same thing; we're parts of the same whole, a higher intelligence somewhere out there. You can call it whatever you want: God, creator, the infinite, Source, the universe, life-force energy. Source works best for me. This Source is pure love, pure light, pure creative energy. They report that Source wants to experience creation and life, so it breaks off into trillions of souls and sends them out into the worlds to have all sorts of experiences. We as these souls go through different schools, experience the teachings each school has to offer, learn lessons, and expand our consciousness, so that in our next life we have hopefully leveled up and are ready for the next grade of school, the next lesson. We're constantly rising in our level of consciousness, ascending the ladder back to Source. Death is merely a transition where we get to take off the human masks we have been wearing and return to our true form.

In this place between lives, we find out where we go next. We've either learned the lessons we were meant to in our most recent life or we must repeat them. If we repeat them, we reincarnate again into a similar type of life until we learn them. Once we learn them, we move on to a different lesson in another school. Sometimes we incarnate on Earth, sometimes we incarnate elsewhere. But we are still the essence of ourselves. That never changes. Between each lifetime, we go over what we learned in our last life, and we remember everything—all of our past lives, where we came from, what lessons we were supposed to learn—and can look at our most recent experience as a human being from an objective place without the emotions and lens of the human life we had most recently lived.

When it's time for you to move to your next life, you help to pick the life you will have. It's like a video game where you pick your avatar and the level of difficulty. You choose your country, the parents you will be born to, what you look like, the big life circumstances that will be thrown your way, and the way you will die, because those choices will best help create the circumstances around you to catapult your growth. They set the stage for you to learn the lessons you're meant to learn next. They ready the soil, plant the seeds. Then it's up to you if you grow.

I know that this is a hard pill to swallow, and if right now you're thinking something like, "Sure, it's easy to say that from a place of privilege," stick with me. I respond to this challenging thought in a later chapter.

For now, ask yourself, "What if this *is* true? How would this knowledge change the way I live my life?"

Remember, you can just pretend I'm telling you an incredible story. And just because this might be different from what you were taught doesn't mean it has to be one or the other. Maybe there's a way for the two ideas to coexist harmoniously.

You don't have to make up your mind about anything right now. As you simply continue reading, a corner of your mind will start to open to new possibilities and ideas as your subconscious absorbs the words. There is a part of you that knows the truth deep down, a part of you that remembers and is ready to be awakened. The fact that you've picked up this book at all tells me you're looking for answers and already on a path to awakening. So try not to worry too much about details that don't feel right and instead soak up the whole thing like a sponge. The drops not meant for you will fall away.

Once you start to realize that you are this divine being here to have as many experiences as is earthly possible and you never really die—you just transition back into your true form—it takes the pressure off and a bit of fear starts to fade away. Because the truth is, nothing can hurt you because you are eternal. You are energy. And nothing in this lifetime is so scary, or should be taken so seriously, because at the end of this play, the curtain will rise, and the actors will take off their costumes, and you will realize you were just playing the lead role. You start to realize that taking risks can bring tremendous rewards, and that if you don't take risks, you won't grow as exponentially. Just like how Neo learned in the first *Matrix* movie that he could bend time to dodge bullets and punch through walls because they weren't as solid as he'd thought they were, when you start to view life as a play and a school, you realize the rules you once thought were hard and fast are in fact malleable and things are not quite as they appear.

A Million Pieces of You

Since I'm introducing you to mind-bending ideas you might not have ever been exposed to before, I'd like to take this even a step deeper and introduce the concept that maybe you are not a complete and whole soul. Maybe you are a fraction of a soul. Stay with me here.

Dolores Cannon uncovered that the best way for you to have the most experiences is to have multiple versions of you. So there are a million versions of you existing across time lines on this planet in parallel lives. Every time you make a choice, a new time line branches out and a parallel life is started where the other version of you makes the other choice. So one version of you chose the choice you did, and another version of you chose the other choice. Soon each of those time lines split off into two more branches the next time those versions of you have to make a choice, and so on and so on. So there are practically an infinite number of plays—time lines—starring you, right now, as the lead actor. Some of the time lines are incredibly similar to the one you're consciously living now and some of them are vastly different. So one version of you is still with your ex, one version of you may be single, one version of you is with someone you've never even met before, one version of you has kids, one version doesn't. There is already that version of you who has that job you feel too afraid to go for in this lifetime. There's a version of you who took that leap of faith or that opportunity that you passed up. And somewhere, in this vast place known as the universe, a version of you has exactly what you want now.

The purpose of this is so that you can collect as many experiences while you are a human being as possible to take back to Source, so that when all of these fractions of a soul come back together after this lifetime, you'll have a huge wealth of combined experiences and life lessons that you have learned.

Quantum Physics backs this up. *The Many-Worlds Interpretation of Quantum Mechanics* says there are many parallel worlds and universes that exist at the same time and in the same space as our own and that all possible outcomes are physically realized in these other worlds. Remember the double-slit experiment and how it taught us that electrons (matter) are waves but appear to us as particles once we measure and observe them? Quantum Physics tells us that before we measure those electrons, they exist on a wave function—think of it like a cloud or a realm of possibilities—and could be in any possible place within that cloud. Once we measure or observe the electron, the wave function "collapses" and we see the electron as a particle in one point in time and space only. *The Many-Worlds Interpretation* says that all of those other possibilities of where the electron could be within the cloud each exist in a different world from our own—in a parallel reality.

Gregg Braden explains in *The Isaiah Effect* how everything we know in our world is made up of the same thing: tiny packets of light called quanta that vibrate at different speeds. The speed in which they vibrate dictates what they appear to us as. He explains that rocks and minerals are made up of light that vibrates very slowly. The living material of plants, animals, and humans are made up of light vibrating at a faster rate. Even more rapidly vibrating light makes up television and radio signals. He goes on to explain that shortly after the moment of creation, the universe was expanding so quickly that 90 percent of it vibrated way past the three-dimensional experience we are living in and into much higher states of expression. He posits that the parallel universes of the many-worlds theory live in this 90 percent.

Remember how we only can see 0.0035 percent of the light spectrum? The other 99.99 percent of the world around us is invisible? Who's to say these other time lines and dimensions are not laid on top of ours like transparencies and all happening simultaneously?

This way of thinking is comforting to me because I know that it's completely possible to get the things I want. It also makes me take life and my perceived problems a little less seriously. For a while, I was having trouble conceiving children but knew some other version of me had them and was living through the challenges and the joys and the learnings and the love and the triumphs of having them. Knowing they're out there, somewhere, made it feel okay that I didn't have them in this lifetime.

Open your mind and shift your thinking. I know it's all mind-boggling to really think about. But ask yourself if somewhere in all of this, you don't feel a hint of truth. Maybe it's the goosebumps running down your arms, or the way your heart started to beat just a little faster as you were reading about it. Maybe there's a part of you that feels this to be true. It's hidden, sacred knowledge. You've forgotten, but you're starting to remember. Life isn't happening *to* you, it's happening *for* you.

It makes chasing your dreams a little less daunting, doesn't it? There's probably a version of you out there who is outgoing where you have social anxiety because they've learned to overcome it. A version of you who is a go-getter and has jumped at every opportunity life threw their way and because of it they are highly successful. The possibilities are truly endless. In the end, you all converge back and all of that knowledge is shared. What will you share from the experiences of your life?

Change your mind around what is possible, what you're capable of, and what is really holding you back from becoming the greatest version of you that you possibly can be. You literally have nothing to lose.

And beyond that, all of the possibilities of what you can have already exist in the quantum field. Every possible choice exists—everything you can imagine and everything you can't. It's out there, available to you. Nothing is impossible or too far-fetched. You simply have to vibrate at the frequency of the thing you want to call into existence in *your* time line. You have to align with it.

Quantum Physics tells us that within the universe exists an infinite number of overlapping possibilities, and that the versions of our bodies, our lives, our circumstances, and our planet that we see in our daily lives only exist because they were chosen from this vast realm of possibilities. Each possible future version lays out there in a state of rest until it is chosen. So if we want to change something in our lives, we need to consciously choose that new version. As we imagine how we want our future to look—as we use the Law of Attraction—we then call that future into existence through the conscious choices we're making in the present.

You are allowed to change your mind and reinvent yourself at any time. Like the Hawk character from the TV show *Cobra Kai*. He is a nerdy kid who gets picked on and made fun of. He leaves his karate dojo one day after getting picked on, and you think he's just running home to cry like he has in the past. But the next day he shows up with a blue mohawk and punk rock clothes and a new attitude to match it. He changed his mind and reinvented himself and becomes one of the toughest kids whom everyone respects. He changed his reality.

Up until 2017, I was working in the bustling tech industry in the Bay Area of California. I was climbing the ladder in the marketing world. I had been head of marketing at a small start-up for years and loved my job and my coworkers. When that company closed its doors because we lost funding, I was devastated, but then I found another job as head of digital marketing for a larger tech start-up that was well funded. The commute was closer to my house, along the water in the Jack London neighborhood of

Oakland. I could see the iconic Oakland cranes in the distance that were George Lucas's inspiration for the AT-AT Walkers in *Star Wars*. I was making a six-figure paycheck. On paper, everything looked perfect. Inside, I was reeling. I started having panic attacks every night but had no idea what they were from. Finally, other physical issues started popping up, and my good friend who is a functional medicine doctor tested me and found out I had Hashimoto's, an autoimmune disease where your immune system attacks your thyroid gland.

During this time, I had also decided to take yoga teacher training. During the week, I would go to my job, then I spent Friday evening to Sunday evening at teacher training. From the moment I walked into TT that first night, I felt at home. Like I was right where I was supposed to be. I was surrounded by like-minded people, learning about pranayama and chakras and trying all types of yoga. Everyone was open and real and allowed themselves to be vulnerable and do the hard inner work. I could talk about all the things I loved talking about. It was beautiful. But then the dreamy weekend would end and I would be back at work and having panic attacks in the evenings again until the next weekend would roll around.

When the Hashimoto's disease diagnosis came, it clicked. I knew it was a sign that I wasn't where I was meant to be and wasn't doing what I was supposed to be doing. I felt like the universe had been poking at me with the panic attacks, trying to get my attention. Like, "Hey. Hey, you. Hey. Over here!" But I had just ignored it. So it took me by both shoulders and shook me hard to make sure I couldn't ignore the message. Sometimes the universe wants you to move in order to discover the path you're meant to go on, and if you're not moving, it will make things so uncomfortable and painful on your current trajectory that you have no choice but to move.

I had been sitting in yoga teacher training and watching my two trainers for the past five weeks while thinking about how cool their job was. Much to my dismay, they told us that no one else besides them had full-time jobs as yoga teachers at that company. I was told it was hard to make it as a yoga teacher. You had to hustle and market yourself and would end up barely scraping by. I just knew in my heart I could make it in a way that I could pay my bills, though. Halfway through teacher training, I took a leap of faith. I left the tech world and my six-figure paycheck to follow my dreams of becoming a yoga teacher. I wholeheartedly believed it would happen, so I trusted and took the step. And I went on to become a studio manager and finally Director of West Coast Operations at the company where I made $60,000/year. That certainly isn't six figures, but it's the national average salary and practically unheard of in the yoga industry, and it was much better than barely scraping by like I had been told would happen. With the promotion to director also came the responsibility of running teacher training. In two short years, I was doing the job of the trainers whose job I had admired.

Stepping outside of your comfort zone is of the utmost importance because that's where growth happens. You might have heard the phrase, "The comfort zone is where dreams go to die." When I signed up for yoga teacher training, I had never done anything like that before. I had never put my body through its paces and challenged myself physically and mentally like that. But it opened up a whole new world of possibilities. I grew in confidence and toughness as well as in yoga ability, public speaking, and leadership skills. I healed a lot of past trauma, as well. My mind was stretched along with my body, and you know what they say about stretched minds. Once they're expanded, they can never go back to where they used to be. You are changed forever by new experiences.

Just consider for a moment that all of this is true. How do we harness that power within us to bend these rules of nature? The answer is through the thoughts we think. All you have to do is change your mind to change your reality.

CHAPTER 3

FLIPPING YOUR INNER DIALOGUE

So if we have this amazing magical power, then why do so many people fail at creating the life they desire?

The answer is your ego, which is that small (sometimes not so small) voice in your head. The voice of doubt. The voice of "reason." The cynic. The critic. The "realist." The one that says when your heart wants to go for a new job, "You're not qualified. You'll never get it. And if you do get it, it'll be hard and you'll be in way over your head. Best to stay where you're at, where you're comfortable. You're doing good where you are now. Why ruin a good thing?"

The ego is kind of like the computer software that comes with being human. It doesn't know you are a vast, powerful, spiritual being. All it sees is a body and a mind. It runs programs based on fear and doubt and worry in order to protect the body because it identifies with the body and the mind. It's the part of you that thinks you are your body and you are your mind even though you are so much more. So it does everything it can to keep you safe in a way that it believes will keep you safe.

When you believe that you are a body only, it makes you very vulnerable and at the mercy of the world. There is danger all around you and so much that is beyond your control. Each time you get in your car, board a plane, step out of your house after dark, or expose yourself to the elements you must be on high alert. In a world where public shootings, nuclear war, diseases, natural disasters, and more are very real possibilities that can end your life in a flash, it's easy to see how ego believes it must protect and defend you at all times and must always be on the offense.

The ego doesn't understand that your body is merely an avatar; it has bought into the illusion of reality. Anything it can't perceive, it doesn't think is real. And anything it experiences through its five senses it calls real life. But because it only sees this restricted view of reality, it is limited to a small piece of the whole and thus limits you. Your true potential extends so much further beyond these imaginary limits.

As we grew up, the adults in our life rewarded us when we behaved a certain way and punished us when we behaved another way. At their core, all human beings want to be loved, and when we got rewarded, we felt loved. Soon we started to fear doing bad things because not only were we afraid of punishment, but we also were afraid that we wouldn't be loved.

Think back on what you were taught growing up. From the time we were little kids, not only were we rewarded and punished, but we were also graded, compared, judged, and evaluated on every aspect of our lives. Rather than living in the moment and being content and happy with who you are, life became a constant competition for the best test scores, the winning sports team, your crush's attention, your parents' approval, the most likes on social media, the best job, your boss's recognition, the biggest paycheck, the nicest house, the trendiest clothes, the coolest entertainment collection, and even the most unique personality or best sense of humor. Think about being on a dating app, where you're literally shopping for a potential partner, and how everyone is trying to stand out as original and the best. It seems that everywhere we look from the TV to our families to social media to our schools to our jobs, it's all about competition and comparison. And since we're taught these things from a young, impressionable age, they start to form our inner judge, our inner critic, our lens, and the voice inside of our head that we talk to ourselves with. They shape the way we see the world.

We fit ourselves into a mold—the mold of what society said we were "supposed" to be like, act like, look like, dress like, and talk like. Even the things we wanted and cared about, like what we should be when we grew up, were the design of this mold. We adopted the beliefs, habits, and thoughts of the adults in our world and, as we grew older, the people we admired, like the popular classmate in school or our favorite actor, until we looked like carbon copies of them. We even mimicked their voice and the catchy sayings and slang they used. The more we conformed to this idea of becoming others, the less we became ourselves. After a while, our ego became developed enough and we started punishing ourselves more than anyone else in our life did. We started feeling guilt or shame if we did something wrong. We started feeling stressed if we were not liked. We felt unworthy if we got rejected. We felt fear at the idea of following our dreams and really living. Human beings are pack animals at their heart—we all want to be wanted and included, and ego told us that leaving the pack could be dangerous or even deadly. These inherited beliefs ruled our lives so much that we also started to judge anyone else who did not abide by them. We held others and ourselves to such high expectations, and if we failed to meet them, we beat ourselves up so much.

Life as a modern human being becomes so complex and fitting within the mold becomes so all-consuming that pretty soon it is all we know, all we focus on, all we care about. Add on top of these internal pressures and expectations advertisements from major companies, every type of flashy entertainment you could imagine, alarming news segments, and more loud external factors all trying to distract you and grab your attention and pull you in a million different directions. Connecting to your inner being became like trying to look at only one thing in the middle of the Las Vegas strip. It's easy to see how ego takes over and makes us lose sight of who we really are.

Your true self, the powerful spiritual being that you are, is perfect exactly as you are. The version of you that you show up as in any given moment is perfect. You are worthy. You are enough. You are whole. You are deserving. You are loveable. You are complete and lacking nothing. Everything placed on top of you—losses, failures, accomplishments, wins—is all meaningless in the long run because it's all completely subjective. You've either decided that it's so or you've listened to someone else's opinion that it's so. Opinions come and go, are fleeting. A scandal might be big news one day and forgotten about a week later. You make yourself vulnerable and easily affected when you identify so strongly with, and take so seriously, the opinions of others. Each person on Earth is on their own mission to bring their unique gifts to humanity. There's no need to compete or compare yourself to anyone else.

The ego thinks we are separate from the rest. That everyone is an individual and life is a competition. It thinks that someone can't get something good without someone else getting something less. It sees lack instead of abundance. It sees things in black and white. It believes things are either good or bad, painful or pleasurable. It panics. It fears. It feels guilt. It places blame. It judges. It feels jealous. It plays the victim. It believes in suffering.

The ego isn't there to make you depressed or feel bad about yourself, even if that is sometimes the result. It's there to protect you. At least, it thinks it's protecting you. It tries to keep you safe by never moving, never growing. The ego thinks that if you don't leave your comfort zone or take risks, you can't get hurt. What the ego doesn't realize is that by leaving your comfort zone, taking action steps toward your goals, believing and trusting wholeheartedly to the point of even doing things that scare you, your dreams can actually materialize.

Now I don't want you to hate your ego because it serves a very important purpose. It's great at protecting you from not walking off a cliff or getting out of the way of oncoming traffic. And it's a part of being human. Everything about you is perfect, whole, and complete and there's no part of you that's broken. The ego just doesn't need to take the steering wheel in matters of the heart and oftentimes we tend to let it because we don't know any better, because we identify with it and think that it is us.

So, if our true selves are spiritual beings and we're just here on Earth pretending to be human beings for a bit while we learn how to use our powers, then how do we rise above all of this earthly drama? How do we step out of this whirlwind?

The answer is by changing our minds and our beliefs, learning what we were meant to learn, and the first step is becoming conscious and accepting of your true purpose so that you can then begin removing the obstacles keeping you from achieving that purpose.

Your Thoughts Are Powerful Messengers

When I was in my mid-thirties, my husband and I were doing IVF. For as long as I could remember, IVF was one of my biggest fears. I remember being fifteen years old and saying I would never give myself shots in the stomach. I don't know why that had even entered my fifteen-year-old consciousness as a possibility, but I have to believe that I either manifested it or it's some sort of life lesson I needed to work out.

We were finished with the rounds of shots, and the day of egg retrieval when a doctor would perform a minor surgery to remove all of the eggs you've been growing from your ovaries was fast approaching. It had been this big, looming thing in my mind for weeks now. Getting put under was one of my fears, and the night before, I felt like I was in full panic mode. I think I was so scared of getting put under because I had no control in the situation. I would literally be unconscious. It was yet another lesson in relinquishing control and trusting in the universe.

I fell asleep fine that night but woke up at 4:50 am and couldn't sleep. Rather than panicking, I laid in bed with my eye mask on, imagining my future family. I could see my children and picture their faces so clearly. I knew what their names would be and what their personalities were like and what hobbies they'd love. I imagined our life together in a way that was so vivid, it was like I was watching home movies projected onto the backs of my eyelids. Then I started manifesting the egg retrieval going perfectly and quickly and easily and that I would be calm in the morning. I laid there thinking about that for about an hour before I drifted back into sleep.

To my shock, when I woke up again, I was full of joy. I was feeling good and *so* happy. It was like I was buzzing and on another plane. I couldn't stop smiling. Shane suspiciously watched me, waiting for the other shoe to drop. He had been prepared to comfort me but instead left confused and probably cautiously relieved.

I was calm on the drive to the clinic and as we waited together in the little room that was sectioned off with curtains. I just trusted the universe. What was interesting, though, was that I was really noticing my thoughts, and while negative, fear-based thoughts tried to creep in, I just kept saying no and scraping them out of my consciousness as if I was placing a barrier there. I started imagining those table scrapers servers use to clear away table crumbs, and every time a negative thought would come, I would scrape it away. *"Not today and not ever again. I have no time for you,"* I told them in my head. And it worked every time! It was so easy to see how they were trying so hard to invade me. I've heard that when fear is really showing up like that, you're just on the edge of your breakthrough and the ego is trying to make a last stand. I felt like my life had changed. I didn't need to allow those thoughts in. I could stay in a state of joy, a happy place, and put up a security perimeter even though they kept trying to invade. When you scrape aside the fear-based thoughts, all that is left will be the golden shining light of possibility. Notice your thoughts and believe that you can and should consciously direct them rather than leave them to the ego that is less aware than you are.

Define the Messages Revealed by Your Thoughts

Rather than just roaming pieces of information floating in and out of your conscious mind, view your thoughts as powerful tools. Start paying attention to your thoughts. You can use your thoughts to figure out what you want, where you are unfulfilled, and what you are fearful of. Some of your thoughts, of course, will be things like what you're going to have for dinner and can be disregarded for this purpose. But thoughts that fall into one of these three categories—your wants, your fears, and where you're unfulfilled—are giving you a wealth of information about your purpose, passion, and joy in life. Pay close attention to what they are telling you rather than just reacting to them.

As you go about your day, start to notice your thoughts and write them down into the three categories. Carry a small notebook with you or do it in a notes app in your phone so you can use these lists later on.

Thoughts about what you want feel like daydreaming about what could be, what you wish you had, what perhaps you see others have that you want. It's a pulling at your heart strings, a longing for something so bad you ache for it. If you find yourself wishing you could meet the partner of your dreams, that is a thought showing you what you want. Sometimes thoughts can do double duty. If you find yourself daydreaming about becoming a famous actor instead of being stuck in your dull desk job, you can file that under the Want and Unfulfilled columns.

Unfulfilled thoughts show up as unhappiness, uneasiness, frustration, restlessness, anger, or disappointment about current life circumstances. Every thought that feels like a complaint belongs in the Unfulfilled column. If you notice you're groaning to yourself about having to get out of bed to go to work and feel like you're really having to drag yourself there, that thought might be revealing that you're not satisfied with your current job. If you find yourself complaining internally about your paycheck or feeling jealous of a coworker who got a raise, that might be a sign that you're unfulfilled with your compensation.

The third type of thought to pay attention to represents your fears. Fear-based thoughts keep you in lack, in competition with others, in running out of time, in doubting your abilities, and in feeling insecure, and leave you feeling stressed and anxious. They are constricting rather than expanding. Are you constantly worried about losing your job? Do you feel nervous about a conversation you have to have with someone? Are you anxious about the behavior of your significant other? Are you stressing about a mole you found on your back? Write these down under the Fears column.

Emotions like jealousy are good determiners of what you want or where you're feeling unfulfilled and might also be fear-based thoughts. If you're unsure of which column or columns to note them, ask yourself why you are feeling jealous. Getting down to the root of it can often give you the clarity you need.

Thoughts can tell you a lot about your state of mind. We're so used to them streaming in and out subconsciously, but they really affect and direct our lives when we react instead of act purposefully, so it's important to shine the light on them and bring them into the conscious state. As you write them down, you'll start to find your mind doesn't need to carry them anymore and may start to obsess about them a little less. You'll also find there will be more space in your mind for the good thoughts. As you write these things down, thank them for showing you what you need to release and then allow them to dissipate. Keep these lists close by, as we'll utilize them a bit later.

Replace Mindless Chatter with Mindful Mantras

You might have noticed how your subconscious mind can just flood thoughts in as a stream of consciousness. Have you ever started thinking about one thing and then before you know it, you've wound up on a topic that is so far away from it and then you traced back the trail of how you got there? Or maybe your mind always goes to worst case scenarios?

There's a way in which we can use this mindless chatter to our advantage and reprogram our brain to let our wandering mind work for us. I like to think of this as casting spells. It's called spelling because that's what we're doing, literally casting spells out into the universe. We just don't always realize it. The words you use when you speak and write and the thoughts you think are constantly helping to shape the reality you live in, the circumstances that "happen to you," and the world you see around you.

Words have more of an effect than you previously realized. Japanese author Masaru Emoto even claims this happens at a microscopic level to elements as natural as water. Emoto took drops of water and put them in containers labeled with words and phrases like love, thank you, peace, harmony, soul, and compassion. Under a microscope, he said that the water crystals took on beautiful symmetrical patterns, each unique as a snowflake. Then he wrote words and phrases like anger, I hate you, sad, and fear on other containers. He interpreted the water crystals under a microscope then to be deformed, discolored, and sloppy. The human body is made up of 60 percent water. If these words can have such a profound effect on a single drop of water, just imagine the effect they can have on you.

What helped me curb my stream-of-consciousness thinking twenty years ago was to replace this mindless chatter with purposeful mindful mantras. I literally trained myself by repeating a mantra every time I caught my mind starting to wander. My mantra is "love, truth, beauty, trust, harmony, peace," which I got from Drunvalo Melchizedek's book *The Ancient Secret of the Flower of Life*. In 2008, I got the words tattooed on me. I repeated that mantra so often that now, when my mind wanders, it automatically repeats that mantra without me having to even think about it. It became second nature. I literally reprogramed my brain, and if I can do it, so can you!

Another excellent way to train your brain is by practicing gratitude. Usually we feel grateful for something *after* we receive it, so feeling gratitude for something you want puts you into a future state and tricks your brain into believing that you've already received it. It automatically puts you on a higher frequency and is an incredible way to instantly transport you into the frequency of abundance. There, it'll be easier for even more things you'll be grateful for to flow your way.

What you think about is what the universe sends you more of. If you're feeling gratitude for the things about your life that you love, and you're in a state of abundance because of that, then the universe will send you more things that are on that same frequency.

Switching to this framework of gratitude is also an excellent way to redirect your thoughts. For example, any time you catch yourself noticing something negative or judgmental about someone else's body or comparing theirs to your own, redirect your attention back to your own body and say to yourself, *Thank you so much for my body. I am so so thankful and so so grateful for my body. I think that my body is beautiful and perfect, right now, exactly as it is.*

As human beings, we can certainly admire beauty in another person. But remember that our ego is constantly forming thoughts about the way in which we view the world, so we're either focusing on what we want or where we're feeling unfulfilled. By using that knowledge to powerfully propel us back into a state of gratitude, we're helping to appreciate and manifest the body that we want.

Another mantra I love to use is what I call my walking mantra. I love taking long walks, which are another form of meditation for me, and I like to say and visualize this while I'm walking:

> *I choose to open myself up to receive love, light,*
> *and healing energy from the universe, and source,*
> *and all life everywhere.*

As I say this to myself, I imagine a pillar of white light about six inches in diameter coming straight down into the top of my head.

> *I choose to allow that love, light, and healing*
> *energy to fill me up until every cell of my being is*
> *vibrating at its frequency.*

At this part, I visualize the white light seeping into every nook and cranny of my body and feel vibration and buzzing! I get goosebumps every time.

> *I choose for that love, light, and healing energy*
> *to spill over into my light body and energy body until*
> *my entire physical body, light body, and energy body*
> *are filled with the love, light, and healing energy*
> *from the universe, source, and all life everywhere.*

Here, I visualize that white light spilling beyond me into a big bubble that encompasses me and is around eight feet wider than me on every side.

> *I choose to open up my heart and send out*
> *love, light, and healing energy to my beautiful and*
> *amazing planet Earth and to all life on her and all*
> *life everywhere.*

I imagine a new pillar of white light now coming out of my chest, out into the world.

> *I choose to open myself up to be a channel of*
> *love, light, and healing energy, allowing the love,*
> *light, and healing energy to flow through me while*
> *always keeping the exact amount of love, light, and*
> *healing energy for myself that I require.*

I visualize and feel the entire flow—the white light coming into the top of my head, circulating through my body, pouring out past my body, and shooting out of my heart space in one continuous flow.

Right now, and it is so.

Finally, I visualize millions of lightworkers connecting across the globe until it's filled with light. Each one as a tiny point of white light sending out a stream of white light in an arc, which meets another tiny white dot of a lightworker and so on until Earth is covered in a grid. I am usually buzzing and feeling so much love and lightness and joy by the time I am finished.

Another one I like to say often is, "I choose love, truth, beauty, trust, harmony, peace, light, and happiness for my beautiful and amazing planet Earth and all life on her and all life everywhere." And I try to feel the feelings of those emotions and hold that beauty and that light and all the others. Can you imagine how the world would change if everyone said this mantra even just once per week?

You don't have to use my mantras. In fact, I encourage you to come up with your own instead, something that rings true to you and makes your heart feel joyful and light. The point is to catch yourself every time your mind starts to wander and replace it with the positive mantra of your choosing. You can write it out and put it somewhere in your home or as the background on your phone to remind you of it always.

Our inner dialogue, whether stemming from our ego or our subconscious mind, can have a very real effect on our day-to-day life, and it's important to recognize it for what it is so we can then use it to our advantage. Our inner dialogue is just as important as the language we use externally as we go about our day, whether that's speaking out loud or through the written word. We already know to take care to form our thoughts into words for the external purposes, so now apply that logic to how you treat your inner dialogue. Be purposeful and harness the power of your thoughts by reprogramming your brain to act in the ways you choose rather than react in the ways your ego suggests.

CHAPTER 4

MANIFESTING IN
DAY-TO-DAY LIFE

I've manifested every job I've ever gotten and every salary down to the exact penny. I just wholeheartedly believed that what I'm manifesting would come true and didn't allow a shadow of doubt in my mind, and it has come true every time. When I got hired at my last job, my about-to-be boss told me the amount he would pay me and said, "This is what all of our managers make. This is what the person who you're replacing made." He left no room for negotiation. And it was $10,000 less than I had written down. A little bummed out, I accepted it because I really wanted the job and hung up the phone. I was a little disheartened that my manifesting hadn't worked for once but shook it off and forgot about it and dove into my work. A couple of weeks later he called me out of the blue and told me that he could already tell I was the best hire he had ever made and he was raising my salary by $10,000, to the exact amount I had manifested. I was awe struck.

If you want to truly manifest all of your dreams into reality, you have to fully embody them. One of the best and quickest ways to start calling your desires into your life is to completely and totally envelop yourself in the process. Be intentional with your thoughts, be intentional with your words, be intentional with your writing, be intentional with your environment. In some significant way, align everything you do and everything in your life toward the goal of manifesting. This might sound overwhelming, but just like anything, by breaking it down into several small bits, it quickly amounts to a greater whole. We've already covered how to use your thoughts as manifesting tools, so now let's take a look at things you can do in your outer world.

Put Yourself in the Right Frequency

Getting your home involved is one of the best ways to go about making meaningful change since your home is your refuge, your sacred space where you spend so much of your time.

Each year on January 1, Shane and I write out a short list of our intentions for the year and tape them to our bathroom mirrors. Then each morning and night as we're brushing our teeth and any time we go to wash our hands for the entire year, we're seeing our intentions list. This can just be a really simple list of your overarching goals for the year. They might read something like: Find and get dream house, make $100,000, take a trip with friends, go for a walk every day, and so on.

At the end of December, we take down our lists and write new ones. And guess what? At least 90 percent of the things we wrote down came true by the end of the year. Every single year.

Another fun hack: think about things you type often or think often in your mind. How can you spin them to help you manifest your dreams? You can get really creative here! One thing I do is make all of my passwords into something positive. Since I am typing them all out multiple times each day, they might as well be helping me manifest my dream life.

Other ways to get your home involved can mean physically making space for something you want. Looking to attract a baby into your life? Make a nursery. You don't have to go crazy overboard and buy all of the furniture, but empty out the room and closet, don't use it for something else, and start to refer to it as "the baby's room."

Everything you eat, read, watch, and listen to becomes your diet. Fill yourself up with high vibration entertainment. Avoid things that make you feel fear about the world or make you feel bad and instead spend your time learning about, eating, and watching things that make you feel good. Keep adding to your pile of goodness. When you feel emotions such as fear or anxiety while watching a scary movie or the news, the universe doesn't know the difference between that and your life. It only recognizes the vibration of the emotion. So you're going to attract more of that emotion into your life. Remember that the emotions you feel are some of the strongest ways to manifest into your life and get on the vibration of the thing you want. This is why some actors fall into depression or struggle while playing villains. They spend months or years putting themselves in the state of mind of the character they're playing, so much so that they start to vibrate at that energy and attract it into their lives.

Become absolutely obsessed with the thing you want. If you're trying to manifest the house of your dreams, watch HGTV, browse home Pinterest boards, look at house listings on real estate sites, Google house layouts and plans, draw out your own house plan, and go to stores and look at fixtures that you would love to have in your home. Let your life start to revolve around it.

And lastly, fake it until you make it. Act as though you already have it. This is the very best way to put yourself in the frequency of the thing you want. Feel the emotions of having it. What would you feel like if you had that dream job? *Feel* those things! Feel the excitement of getting the job offer and telling all of your friends and family about it. How would you dress to go into work? Dress that way! Feel the gratitude of having it. Put yourself in the frequency of having it and fully believe it, as if playing a trick on yourself, and watch how quickly the universe delivers it to you.

Journal Your Plan

One of the most powerful ways to launch your dreams forward into reality is to write them down. There's something about putting pen to paper and naming the thing you want that puts the universe into accelerated motion. It also psychologically cements the thing in your brain. You've got a plan, a North Star. It's the way that I've manifested everything in my life—my husband, every job I've ever gotten, the exact temperature on the day of my wedding, and so on.

I recommend getting a brand new journal that you only use for manifesting. Pick one out that feels special to you. Keep it on your bedside table so it's nearby. The best times to manifest are first thing in the morning and right before you go to sleep at night, when you are closest to a relaxed, creative state. Make the space where you write feel special too. Keep it clean. Put a few items around you that make you feel inspired, like a crystal, a Himalayan salt lamp, a plant, a picture of a beloved pet… whatever sparks your soul.

Journaling is essential to being able to manifest the small things in our day-to-day life. For example, maybe a job interview comes up and you want to nail it. Or maybe a loved one is traveling soon and you want to send some extra protection for their journey. I'm going to teach you a journaling technique for those instances that has worked for me for the past twenty years. This journaling technique can be broken down into three parts:

1. Claiming the thing you want to manifest,

2. Affirming that you already have it, and

3. Feeling gratitude for already having it.

I follow a very specific script every time I journal, and you can totally copy it. Let's say I'm manifesting that my dog lives a long, happy, and healthy life. Here's what I would write:

> I *choose* for my dog to live a long, happy, and healthy life. My dog *is* living a long, happy, and healthy life. *Thank you so much, I am so, so thankful and so, so grateful that* my dog is living a long, happy, and healthy life. Right now and it is so.

I always end with "Right now and it is so" to lock it into the present moment because the universe doesn't know time. It doesn't work so well with that example, but imagine you're trying to manifest your dream job. For all the universe knows, you could be asking to get your dream job five years from now, ten years from now, or tomorrow. The key is to be specific.

Be careful with your words because they are powerful. The language you choose is so, so important so you are not communicating something other than what you mean. For example, I've seen people write, "I want to meet my future husband," when they are journaling. But the word "want" implies a lack in the present moment. And remember that we're aligning with the frequency that we want to manifest, so when you say you want something, you're putting yourself in the frequency of not having it yet. Saying that you choose something is putting yourself in an empowered state and confidently deciding on the thing you're manifesting.

You need to also be careful with double negatives. Saying something like, "I choose to not lose my job," will also be confusing to the universe. The universe only works in straight forwardness, so it will hear "lose my job" even though you said the word "not" in front of it.

Similarly, don't say something like, "I don't have cancer anymore." The universe doesn't register the don't—it just sees that you have cancer now and keeps sending you more. Instead, talk about how healthy you are. Focus on what you want, not what you don't want—the positive side, not the negative.

Also don't say things like "going to." For example, "I am going to have my dream house." Using this type of language implies that it's going to happen sometime off in the future. And if you're constantly saying this, it is constantly going to be out of reach in the future. Instead, try saying, "I have my dream house." Write it in the present moment and keep it simple, straightforward, and to the point.

Specificity is also important. Say "I choose to make $150,000 per year." Don't say "I choose to make a lot of money" or "I choose to get a raise." The universe doesn't know what a lot of money is to you and certainly doesn't understand the difference between $1,500 and $150,000. Be specific.

These are just a few examples of how the language you use can either help or hinder you in creating your dream life. I work with my private coaching clients a lot on language and find that having a third party involved can help point out unhelpful language that has slipped into the subconscious.

Putting yourself fully in the state of already having it means getting your emotions involved. Think about how you would feel if you already had that thing. Would you feel energetic? Full of joy? Full of relief? So full of happiness you could burst? *Feel that feeling* as you're writing it. Trick yourself into believing that it's already here. The universe can't tell the difference between this pretending to have it and you actually having it. It will only see that you are on the frequency of having the thing and will deliver it to your doorstep quickly and with ease.

The last step is to completely surrender control. Don't worry or even think about how it's going to happen. That's up to the universe. And oftentimes it will bring things into your life in a way that you couldn't have even imagined anyway. So just focus on putting yourself on the right frequency and allow yourself to be surprised by how your dreams materialize.

Make it a game and have fun with it. Life *is* fun! You can call into your life *anything* you desire and let go of *anything* you don't desire. When you start to view life this way, it becomes exciting and a total blast. And, the best part is that when you're having fun with it and operating from the vibration of joy, it helps you to attract even more joy to you.

Tune into the right frequency, purposefully and specifically map out your dream life, and you can manifest it to your reality. Everything you want already exists in the quantum realm—every single possibility is out there waiting for you to choose it. Everything is energy, and energy is neither created nor destroyed. It always exists, so everything you want to call into your life is out there waiting for you.

CHAPTER 5

CRAFTING YOUR DREAM LIFE

After eighteen years immersed in the Law of Attraction, I thought I knew how to incorporate it into my life meaningfully. After participating in a virtual dream-building event a few years back, however, I learned a new technique that changed my life. Through Mary Morrissey's instruction, I learned the value of spending time figuring out what I *didn't* know I wanted.

Morrissey explained that the opposite of "great" is "good." A lot of people don't dream bigger because they have become content with what they have or worry that striving for more will "mess up" what they have. They think, *I already have a good house, a good job, a good marriage. Why should I want to change that? If it's not broken, why would I fix it?* Wanting more makes them feel guilty or greedy or unappreciative for what they already have. But it's okay to feel gratitude for what you have while simultaneously reaching for more. You can settle with good, or you can strive for great.

After the event, I thought about my long-held desire to design and build my dream house on several acres with horses and cows and donkeys and chickens, all sorts of rescue animals. I loved our current home. We lived in a great neighborhood in a lovely town. But our house was small and cramped with poor storage space. Both Shane and I had begun working from home, and my office had become the dining room table. I had to face the fact that we had outgrown our small home.

With "good to great" in my mind, I journaled about what my dream home would look like and envisioned it surrounded by rolling hills and beautiful trees. I imagined how many rooms the house would have, the square footage, the design of the kitchen, and what the fixtures would look like. I poured all the detail I could into it.

I asked myself, "What is one step I could take today that would move me in the direction of my dream home?" And so I began scouting property listings for opportunities. Shane and I both love real estate and looking at properties was fun for us, so we started looking at vacant lots. We lived in the Bay Area of California, though, and real estate prices were surging. Most vacant lots we would actually want to purchase were listed way above our price range. If we sold our house, we would have to use all of the profit we made to build, so we couldn't sell our house and afford to buy that expensive property and have leftover money to build. I kept looking though, because I knew taking steps toward my dream house was the only way to manifest it.

Then the right opportunity landed in our laps when members of our family unexpectedly offered us a portion of their acreage out of the blue. They lived on a horse ranch that backed up to

300,000 acres of open space with trails. The next weekend we went to look at the property and it was perfect. The views were beautiful, and there was complete privacy. We would have space to have all the rescue animals I dreamed about.

Finding the property was only the first step. Next came working with the city planning department, an architect, and a civil engineer to see if we could even subdivide the property.

As our plans became more and more solidified, we began to see our dream home come into clearer focus. As the house and property plans were created and we got to put in all of the amazing details we dreamed of, we started to really be able to visualize ourselves living in the house. It became so real we could almost touch it. We visited the site often to daydream about the views from each window, where we would have our morning coffee, and where our future children would play. We imagined taking daily walks on the trails and raising a family surrounded by animals and nature. It became so real that we had no doubts it was going to happen. We didn't have to force the vision. It just felt right. We started referring to it as "our new house" in casual conversation, as if it were already real. We were willing it into being.

Around two weeks before we submitted our plans to the city, both the state of California and the city passed laws that would make it easier and quicker to subdivide property and build because there was such a high demand for housing. The universe was working in our favor once again.

On the day we submitted our materials, Shane and I looked at each other in awe and disbelief at just how awesome this journey had been. We hadn't even been thinking about moving or getting a new house. I had just journaled about it, having no idea how the heck it would actually happen, and suddenly we had codesigned a house that we would really love.

The city ended up approving all of our plans and our new home is on its way to becoming a reality.

It's not selfish or greedy to want things—even if you are content with what you already have. Gratitude and wanting more can coexist. Remember, this is why you're here, to learn how to use your power to manipulate energy. It's your literal birth right to use the power that you have.

The Milkshake and the House

As you start to craft the life you want, start to call in what you desire, and these things begin to appear in your life—maybe slowly at first, in a trickle even—then you'll start to believe in the power you possess more and more. The universe doesn't know the difference between a small- ticket item like a milkshake and a big-ticket item like a house. Only your mind, your ego, assigns a difference there. Because everything is just energy vibrating, for the universe to deliver a house instead of a milkshake takes no extra work or manipulation. It is simply your ego, your fears, your doubts that creep in and whisper, "No, that's impossible. It's too big."

So start small if you need to. Manifest yourself a milkshake. Taste it right now. What flavor is it? Feel yourself sucking on the straw, feel the texture of it in your mouth, feel the coldness. Maybe even the brain freeze! Feel the frosty cup in your hand, wet and cold with condensation. And now feel how you would feel as you take that first sip. Would you feel joy? Would it take you back to your childhood? Would you feel the sugar rush? Now journal on it. And completely let go of the "how" it's going to happen. Trust in the universe that this milkshake will be brought into your life. Chances are it'll find its way to you in a completely surprising way you couldn't have possibly predicted. Maybe you'll be walking down the street and a store will be giving out free milkshakes or a friend will bring one over to your house to surprise you. The only thing you shouldn't do is go out seeking a milkshake. Instead, let yourself be surprised by how it materializes into your life. Watch the magic unfold.

Now you might try this and it will work, and for a moment you'll feel awe and excitement, but then your ego, your thinking mind, may quickly come in and say something like, "Yeah, but that's just a milkshake. It could just be a coincidence. I want to be able to build my dream house and that's a much bigger, more expensive ask than a milkshake." That's your doubt filtering in, and it's inevitable that this will happen. That's part of the human experience.

Bigger and Bigger Steps

The best way to expel your doubt is to keep taking bigger and bigger steps. Each time write down something that seems more and more outlandish. Pick things to see or happen to you in your daily life. For example, write down that you'll see a 3-legged orange cat or an old childhood friend will call you. Turn it into a fun hobby. As you do this, and the things you manifest keep materializing into your life, you'll prove it to yourself and the doubt will naturally fall away. Essentially, don't try to talk yourself into anything because it won't work—instead show yourself. Allow yourself to be surprised. After a while it will be hard for ego to keep calling these occurrences coincidences. And as you believe in your power more and more, the stronger your ability to manifest will get. Before you know it, you'll feel limitless in what you can manifest for your life on Earth.

Because you really have two choices: You can either let life happen *to* you or you can design and manifest the life that you want, make life happen *for* you. You can become a victim of your circumstances, feeling powerless and out of control for anything that life throws your way, or you can take your power back and start consciously creating like the powerful being you are. Start to turn on your power and recognize that you are the designer of your own life.

Either way, life is going to keep happening and you are going to keep creating for, well, as long as you live. We never stop creating—it's in our nature. We just do it unconsciously and often end up manifesting that which we fear most because it's what we focus on. It's like running on autopilot instead of taking control of the steering wheel. Even if you're not fully sold yet, you might as well try my way because you've got nothing to lose and a whole lot to gain—the life of your dreams!

Defining What You Want Accurately and Specifically

You have the power to create the life of your dreams that would make you wake up each morning feeling vibrant and energized and full of exuberance, but what if you don't know what you want? What if you don't know what the life of your dreams would really look like?

I'm going to share an exercise that I do with my clients to help them define what they want. Even if you're reading this and thinking to yourself, "I know exactly what I want," try it because you just might discover something you didn't even know you wanted. So in this exercise you're going to break up your life into seven different areas to think about each one of these separately so you can get really clear on your dream.

Grab seven pieces of paper. On the top of each one, write each label: Health, Romance, Relationships, Career, Leisure, Personal Growth, Tangibles. First, rate each area of your life on a scale of one to ten, one being everything is horrible, miserable, you can't go on and ten being everything is perfect, you're living your dream life, you couldn't imagine it any better than it is now. Be honest with yourself.

Now that you know where you really stand in each area of your life, let's focus on getting each of those up to a ten out of ten.

True success, truly rich people, are wealthy in all seven areas of their life. Now someone might look like they're successful from the outside; maybe they're successful on paper. But if they're not fulfilled in all seven areas and feel like something is missing, then they aren't truly rich, truly successful. That's why it's so impossible to judge another person, because we don't know their full story. Just because someone is rich in tangibles like a lot of money, a big house, and a nice car doesn't mean they're not bankrupt in their relationships or their health or any other area of their life.

When you can truly look at all seven areas of your life and rate each one a ten out of ten, then you can call yourself rich and successful. When you have a sense of purpose, when you have passion, when you have love, when you're physically and emotionally healthy, when you wake up each day in love with your life, *that's* real wealth. And this is what is absolutely attainable to you, no matter *what* your current circumstances are.

Truly successful people create the results that they want in their life. The biggest key though? They don't let their fear, doubt, worry, insecurities, envy, and other low vibration emotions get in the way. They don't compare themselves to others. I didn't say they don't have these feelings—of course they do. All human beings feel them at one time or another. But they don't let them hold them back. All truly successful people are only different from unsuccessful people because they have a different mindset, they've created different habits, and they don't let their fear get to them.

Most people live only a fraction of the life they're capable of living. They wake up stressed and worried rather than passionate and excited, staying close to what they consider their safety net and not venturing out of their comfort zone. They think, "Things are pretty good, why rock the boat?" They doubt themselves and their abilities. But we are powerful, spiritual beings, all of us, so everyone has the capability and potential to live a big life, to be successful in all seven areas, and to be outstanding. A lot of people don't even try because of fear. They're afraid of failure, afraid of rejection, afraid of pain, afraid of other people's opinions, and their thoughts hold them back because they stem from these fears. Some don't have the self-awareness to realize this, while others don't have the support to move through and past it. Working with a coach can be so empowering and help you shatter all of the lenses and stories you've built up around yourself, which I know because I've helped so many of my clients have breakthroughs around their unconscious fears.

Have courage. Believe you can, because courage starts in your mind. Once you change your mind, it will surprise you how quickly life will transform for you. When you shift your thinking toward what's possible and truly believe that you are capable and deserving—when you step into your power—doors open up for you and the past no longer has a hold on you. Your old stale beliefs start crumbling and new powerful beliefs start forming.

Your current circumstances and situations are a result of your current thoughts, beliefs, lens, emotions, and habits. As you change these things, as you do the work, the universe rearranges everything around you. Start with the tools and steps you have at your disposal today and trust that, as you keep moving forward, better tools will find their way to you. If you keep thinking that you'll start once something happens (once you get a raise, once your kids are in college, once you pay off your student loans) then you'll be putting it off forever. You don't start once things are perfect. You start where you're at and *you* make things perfect.

Now, take your pieces of paper with your seven categories on them and underneath each header, write a list of everything that would make you rate each category a ten out of ten, so you're creating a list of things you would love to have in each category. I'm not talking about a nice-to-have or a short-term goal—those are best journaled about in the way we covered in previous chapters. Right now I'm talking about things that you would *love*. Things that, if you had them, would make you rate each of the seven categories a ten out of ten.

Allow passion to drive pen to paper and keep judgment out of it. Don't let your ego creep in and say "that's impossible" or try to come up with reasons why it won't work. Just shut your ego out.

When you're sitting down to write out your lists, you must truly suspend all disbelief. Let what you would love pour out of you and onto your paper. Don't try to analyze what you're writing at the same time—it blocks your creative flow. Don't judge. Don't come up with excuses of why what you're writing down "can't" happen. Don't worry about how these things could possibly come to fruition. You can't be in the flow if you are thinking about any of these things Your only task right now is to make your lists based on the life of your dreams.

Here are some examples to get you going:

Health: You might write "I practice yoga every day," "I am completely 100 percent healthy" or "My kidney is functioning at maximum capacity." Now be mindful that you don't want to say something like "My cancer is in remission" because you don't want to take ownership of something like cancer. You don't want to ever own a disease or associate yourself with one because that is a way to claim that thing as yours and the universe will respond by giving you more of it.

Romance: Write down anything you'd like to call into your life when it comes to romance in your life. So you might write "I've met the most wonderful man and he makes me feel so loved," "Jen and I just celebrated our fourth wedding anniversary," or "Sam proposed to me."

Relationships: You can write about any relationships that aren't romantic, such as with family, friends, coworkers, peers, the public, etc.

Maybe you write something like "My brother and I repair our relationship and are closer than ever," "I make a new group of friends who all live within walking distance," or "Everyone at work listens to me and values my opinions."

Career: Write about your job. If you're retired write about how you use your creative talents and skills—maybe in projects around the house or through volunteering. If you're in school, it can be about school. You could write something like "I get promoted to regional director," "I switch careers and open my own flower shop," or "I graduate with honors and get a job offer right away."

Leisure: Leisure is all about hobbies, what you do for fun and recreation. You could say "I'm on a softball league and play once/week," "I take a trip to Paris with my mom and sister," or "I learn to cook gourmet meals." Whatever you enjoy doing and what makes you feel alive.

Personal Growth: This can be any goal you're working toward. Maybe it's that you read twenty-five books this next year. Maybe you sign up for a class to learn a new skill. Maybe you meditate every day. Personal growth and development is such an important aspect of life. If we're not constantly growing and striving to learn new things then we become stagnant, bored, and we lose passion and purpose.

Tangibles: Tangibles are anything that you can physically touch such as a house, a car, money—even a pet dog.

When you think about the tangibles, we must first dispel the thinking that wanting things makes one materialistic or greedy. Remember, desiring things is part of the human experience, and we are here to have experiences as human beings. The trick is to not get so attached to material possessions, that they define you. Getting down to the root of why you want something can give you a lot of insight into your values, purpose, and passion. If you desire more money, consider *why* you might want more money. Maybe it's so you can move somewhere with better schools for your children, or so you can start a company that's going to better the world, or maybe it's just so you never have to do anything that makes you feel like your soul is getting sucked dry again. When you're worried about a paycheck, you will do any kind of work, even if it is constricting rather than expanding for you. Let go of the concept that money is evil. Money isn't evil; rather, it is a tool that allows you to live comfortably enough so you're not in a state of lack and can then focus on giving your gifts to the world. Because it can be challenging to give your gifts to the world if you're worried about where you're going to get your next meal.

For leisure, imagine what you would do if you had all the free time in the world and all the extra money to spend on doing something that would bring you joy.

The universe works with specificity. If you say you want more money, the universe can't send you a check for "more money." It doesn't know what that means because it's too subjective, but it can send you a check for one million dollars. Saying you want to travel more is the same kind of vague. You will still get results, but you could get even better results. For example, if you want to travel, imagine where you would go if there was nothing holding you back. Don't base it on your current circumstances because your dream life doesn't exist on the same frequency as your current life. Keep asking "What else?" until you've got a complete list in each area.

After you're done writing, look at your lists and ask yourself if your vision makes you feel alive and energized when you think about it. That energy factor, the goosebumps on your arms, that excitement building in your chest, that whole body-buzzing sensation… that's the feeling you're going for. That's what's going to put you on the frequency of your dream.

Your Manifest Memoir

Now take all of that detail and write your Manifest Memoir. Pretend that it's sometime in the future, between one and three years. Pick a time frame that feels realistic to you but isn't too far out, no more than three years. Now you're going to write out your Manifest Memoir like you're talking to someone you haven't seen in a while about your amazing life where you now have all of the things you were manifesting. Write in the present or past tense, not the future tense, because remember, in this exercise *you already have all of the things you want*. So keep it in the present moment. Start with the phrase, "I am so grateful that…"

You really want to paint the picture of your dream life to eventually be so real for you that you can easily see yourself living that life. Get all of your five senses involved. What would the thing you want smell like, feel like, look like, and so on.

Don't forget to also add in the emotional aspects. Feel the feelings of what it would be like to live your dream life to give it the energy to manifest into being. When you feel emotions, you send out vibrations and tune to a certain frequency. Emotion also helps put you in the state of it being real right now. And remember, we have to live at the frequency of our dream life. We can't create our dream life from the frequency we operate at now. We have to create from the level of our dream life. Think about how alive and free and full of joy you'll feel once you have all the things you wrote down and make your Manifest Memoir come alive. Paint the picture with images to make it so real that it jumps off the page and so vivid that you can straight up place yourself inside of the scene.

Read this every night before bed. It's a powerful thing to work on manifesting before you go to sleep at night and when you first wake up in the morning because you are closer to an alpha-brain state during those times. That's the state you enter when you meditate and that hypnotists put you in, and you can tap into the universal consciousness so much easier from that place. I like to do it before bed because then I've seeped it into my brain so it can subconsciously work on it while I sleep.

As you read, you are saying the words again, and as you do this over and over every day, you are casting your spell out into the universe.

Keep this Manifest Memoir close by as we'll be back to it in a few chapters and I'll teach you the next step to take. This next step is one of the most important of all. Because while everything you've done up until this moment is important, without this last step you're not going to be able to unlock the life of your dreams.

But first, it's important for us to pivot for a moment to look at forgiveness and healing. Because if we are holding onto or focusing on anger, grudges, pain, guilt, and/or other low-vibration emotions, all of our work so far will be for nothing because those emotions will still unconsciously be driving our life. We have to learn to release these things in order to truly and fully step into our own power and realize our full potential.

CHAPTER 6

PRACTICING FORGIVENESS

Forgiveness is such an essential part of healing, growing, and learning and yet something that is incredibly difficult for most people. It's been difficult for me at times, too. Oftentimes forgiveness requires us to forgive another person without receiving an apology, and our ego steps in and says that they don't deserve our forgiveness or that we need to demand that apology before we could possibly forgive them. But here's the thing: forgiveness isn't for them, it's for you. It's so you can release harmful emotions that you're holding onto.

There's a great Buddhist quote that goes something like, "Holding on to anger is like holding on to a hot coal with the intention of throwing it at someone else. You are the one who gets burned."

Remember that your thoughts create your reality. No one has so much power over you that they can ruin your life, or even your day. Likewise, peace of mind can't be found in blaming other people or events for your suffering. Everything comes from within, from you.

Nothing outside of you ever has the power to take away your peace of mind and happiness. This goes for individuals, groups, circumstances, situations, events, conditions—anything you can think of. People can certainly try. They can spread lies about you, try to humiliate you, criticize you or insult you, and try to make you feel guilt and shame. They can even try to scare, intimidate, and threaten you and physically harm you in some way. But unless you've allowed them to steal your peace and happiness, they cannot. You alone hold that power.

Life is Like a Play and You're the Lead Actor

Because of my work with the Law of Attraction, I was already viewing life as a game. After reading *Between Death and Life* by Dolores Cannon, I started viewing life as a school but also a play. You're the lead character, the people who weave in and out of your life are supporting actors, and the rest of the people in the world are what Dolores calls "background people," like the extras that make scenes more realistic.

Now, many of these prominent actors are individuals you have soul contracts with. If you're not familiar with soul contracts, they are agreements we make with other souls prior to incarnation about something we'll both be involved in together during our next life. I had always thought about soul contracts being between people you care about here, like reincarnating together with your "soul family." But *Between Death and Life* opened my mind up to the idea that you have contracts with other souls, too, who will be involved in big events in your life. These are often friends on the other side of the veil who want to help you grow. They love you so much, and because they love you so much, they agree to play certain parts in your life. Oftentimes they agree to play the villains, because it's the villains who can trigger events in order to inspire us to grow and learn. So these souls love you *so* much that they agree to play this part in your lifetime just so that you can grow, so good can come out of it, even though they know it might be painful for you in the moment. Then, when you both meet again after that lifetime, they'll give you a big hug and tell you they love you and how proud of you they are.

I think about this often when I think about my perceived "enemies"—people who have hurt me throughout my life. Knowing they are some of my biggest cheerleaders on the other side and did to me what they did out of loving kindness, that they love me so much they are willing to let me be angry at them, makes it so much easier to forgive them.

Everyone plays parts in each other's lives. Sometimes you are acting out your soul contract for others and playing the villain in their life. Sometimes people are just background characters in your world. Have you ever been driving and all of the sudden there's all of this traffic out of nowhere, almost like a director said, "Cue the traffic!" and all of these background people suddenly drove to the same street where you are? These moments are for lessons too, maybe to help you work through the emotions of frustration or impatience. Or maybe to make sure you arrive at your destination at exactly the moment you're meant to for some greater purpose.

You Are the Director of Your Story

If all of this seems too far-fetched, then consider that you are in charge of your own story. No one can hurt you in any kind of way unless you decide they can. Any action that someone has taken against you is neutral until your mind gives meaning to it and places the label of "good" or "bad" on top of it. Good and bad are completely subjective. What you might view as harmful, someone else who shared that experience with you might have seen as helpful. You can decide that it doesn't matter. You can decide that good came out of it. You can decide that it was a misunderstanding, or that the other person had good intentions, or that not everything that person brought into your life was negative. *You can change your mind around it.* Be mindful of the stories you tell yourself. Don't talk yourself into a story that isn't true because then it'll harden into a belief and affect your thoughts and forever change the lens through which you view the world.

And the truth is that oftentimes people don't do things just to create chaos and havoc in your life or intentionally hurt you. Just like you have a lens and a story through which you view the world and that drives you to make the choices you make, so does everyone else. If you really knew the big picture, you'd probably only have compassion for them. But because you only see a tiny bit of what's going on, you make all of these assumptions around this person and why they did the things they did. Like *The Four Agreements* says, don't make assumptions and don't take anything personally. That's such a big reason for why we allow people to hurt us, or we perceive that they hurt us, because we take things personally that we shouldn't take personally. Don't take *anything* personally. No one's doing things because of you. They're doing things because of themselves. Everyone's so wrapped up in their own mind, in their own head. They're not worried about what you're doing, while all you're thinking about is how they affect *you*.

Imagine you're sitting in your house when all of the sudden you hear meowing coming from outside. You walk out and find in a corner of your yard a scrawny black and white cat. You go to pet the cat, but it arches its back and hisses at you viciously. You might be frightened of the cat at first or think it's mean or evil. But then suddenly you notice that its back leg is bleeding, then you hear little meows coming from the dark corner behind the cat. You peer over and see four tiny kittens with their eyes still closed, they can't be more than a few days old. Suddenly your perspective shifts from one of fear to one of concern, empathy, and compassion. You can do the same with the people in your life. Try to see things from their perspective. Just like the cat, people who lash out at you in anger, threats, or lies are coming from a place of pain and fear. By extending understanding and the ability to see things from their perspective, not only will you possibly make a friend, but you are teaching that person by your actions. So now they can go out in the world and do the same for someone else. While it may seem the easy route to try to get revenge against someone and lash out in anger and resentment, love and understanding can go a lot further. Both will send ripples out into the world. It's up to you if you send out ripples of hate or ripples of love.

We tend to turn people we perceive to have "done us wrong" into monsters in our minds because it's easier to hate them if we think of them that way. We run everything they've ever said and done through an imaginary filter and rewrite every interaction we've ever had with them into a negative one. We are blinded to all aspects of their personality except for what we see as evil and see ourselves as being far superior to them. And we spend so much energy and effort blaming them for our problems. If you decide that what they did was not evil and you are not bothered by it, then it will no longer affect you. Because the truth is, we don't see things as they are—we see them as *we* are. There's a great quote by sociologist Charles Horton Cooley that goes, "I am not what you think I am. You are what you think I am."[1] We project onto others that which we are still working on in ourselves.

There's likely not a single person in your life whom you love and think is one of the most amazing people ever who hasn't hurt someone else and maybe that other person thinks of your close friend or family member as evil. Chances are, you've even unintentionally or unknowingly hurt some people along the way too. We all make up stories to make ourselves feel better. It's all subjective. And we all have soul contracts with each other. You probably have a soul contract to play the villain in someone's life too.

If you dig down deep and really look objectively at the people you have made into monsters and the situation when you perceived they'd caused you harm, you are likely to find that it was a misunderstanding and be able to see how they perceived the experience from their point of view. As you open your mind up like this, you will also be able to see that they have many redeeming qualities and there are a number of ways they actually helped you grow in your life. You probably grew from

---

1   "Charles Cooley: I Am What I Think You Think I Am," SmartCasualISG, published April 28, 2018, updated January 31, 2021

the situation that happened with them—that is, you *would* grow if you could just let go of your hate.

One of the best ways to learn to forgive and let go is by taking a step back and turning these monsters into other beings you appreciate—into teachers. Mastering the ability to shift your perspective in this way will change your life.

When someone is your teacher, they help you grow. There are two ways to turn monsters into teachers. You have to first recognize the positive attributes that they have. What are some ways they've been kind to you? What are some ways they've helped you? What are some ways they've offered assistance or done something good? What qualities do they have that you admire? Chances are there's something about them that you admire and they have good qualities rather than being the purely evil entity your lack of forgiveness wanted you to believe. It's a matter of sitting down and looking at the person from an objective point of view and taking off the lens you were looking at them through, this story you created around them. When you consider what good they do have inside of them and what good they have brought into your life, chances are you're going to find a lot. Why focus so much on the negative when you could just as easily change your mind and focus on the positive instead?

What good have they brought to others and the world? What do the people who love this person see in them? Everyone has different versions of them, and you get to choose what version of a person you want to focus on. While you might choose to see a negative version, many others will choose to see a positive version. Change your mind about which version you want to focus on, because if you focus on someone's negative attributes, that's the side of them you'll keep getting. If you make the conscious choice to flip your perspective, it can be incredibly illuminating. Not only will your story change around the person, but great healing will take place within you.

Maybe your ego is saying there's nothing good about them, everyone you know hates this individual, and they are liked by no one in this world. If you absolutely can't come up with a single good quality about the person or a single thing you admire or appreciate, then just recognize how they helped you grow. You were in a soul contract with this person, and they've done something that gave you the opportunity to grow. Maybe they've helped you see how you don't want to treat other people, helped you establish more healthy boundaries, or helped you step into your power. Chances are you've learned a lot from them or still could learn a lot. You just have to get past your anger.

If you can learn to see everyone in your life as a teacher, you will always be learning. Every single person you come across in life offers something they can teach you. It's just up to you to open yourself up and be aware of that so you can receive the lesson.

And remember, we are all spiritual beings, pretending to be human beings for a while in this earthly school and we are all parts of the same. Everyone is on a journey, learning lessons and growing. In the grand scheme of things, any earthly drama is likely meaningless once you are both on the other side of the veil and looking back at events from an objective vantage point. Who they are—their personality and looks—when they are incarnated as a human being is a shallow layer and not who they really are.

Rather than being influenced by all these outside factors and people and letting them constantly push your buttons and dictate how you feel, make a conscious choice to feel a certain way. You always have a choice. When you choose to fall into blame and feel like an angry victim, then you're sending that energy out into the universe. In return, the universe is going to deliver more people and circumstances into your life that make you feel angry and like the victim, and the cycle will just repeat. You can decide instead to see the positive outcome, rather than allow yourself to view them how you've been taught you "should" view them. This is your story, and you can easily change it any time you'd like. The script is being written in real time as the play unfolds. When you decide to see how the experience benefited you and made you stronger, smarter, more empathetic, and kinder, then that will be the energy you put out into the universe and the universe will then send you more people who make you feel that way.

Remember, too, that we set up life circumstances for ourselves before we incarnated so that we may grow and learn lessons. If there was something you were supposed to have learned from an experience, you're going to keep getting that same lesson over and over in slightly different ways through slightly different events and people until you finally understand it and respond in a new way. It's up to you to stop the old hurtful pattern from happening again by learning the lesson and growing.

You can easily choose to forgive and not judge others. You don't need to be right or make anyone else wrong. These are mind tricks of the ego and pointless because they just take away your peace of mind. Choose healing rather than blame.

If you're still struggling with this, then think about why you might place blame on others. David R. Hawkins talks in his book *Letting Go: The Pathway of Surrender* about perceived payoffs to blame. When you blame others, you get to claim your own innocence and indulge in self-pity. You also get attention from others: you get showered with sympathy, you get pity for being the victim, and you get honored for being the martyr. When you place blame on others, you get to avoid feeling guilty and stay in your comfort zone of playing small.

What doesn't come from blame, however, is the releasing of negative emotions. You don't get to step into your power and take responsibility for your own healing. You are keeping yourself stuck in the negative loop by reacting to a scenario you interpreted as negative with more negativity. In the long run, this does nothing for you. You do not grow and expand into an even greater soul. You do not find freedom from the exhausting cycle of drama and negativity. Forgiveness is the only way out.

Try making a list of every person that you are holding a grudge against or who has hurt you. Now under each name make a list of every good quality they have and ways that they have helped you out in life. Maybe they taught you something. Maybe they gave you words of encouragement at one point. Maybe they helped you grow.

Now go into meditation and imagine yourself face-to-face with them. Look into their eyes. See their hair, the texture of their skin, the clothes they are wearing. See the soul within their eyes, the magical spiritual being, part of a whole that you are also a part of. Now tell them you forgive them and release them. See them smile when you say that; see the relief cross their face. Give them a big hug. Feel the negative emotions go, and notice the lightness in your being and your own sense of relief as the heavy burden of hatred dissipates.

If you still think the people in your life are unforgivable, I invite you to consider the story of Corrie ten Boom. She and her family were imprisoned in a concentration camp by Nazi soldiers during World War II as punishment for hiding Jews in their home and helping them escape. Her father and sister both died in the camp. She made it out alive and, after the war ended, set up recovery centers for survivors. One day she met a man whom she recognized as a Nazi guard at the camp she had been in who had been particularly cruel to her sister. He asked her for her forgiveness, and she gave it. She felt such a release from that forgiveness that she then spent the rest of her life traveling around the world, teaching others about the power of forgiveness. Forgiveness sets you free.

Nothing Can Hurt Your True Self

You are more than your body, your thoughts, your emotions, your reactions to things. You have a mind, but you're not your mind. You have a body, but you're not your body. You are so much more. Think of it like you have a vehicle or an avatar for this lifetime, which is your body. You may love your body or hate it, but it's your avatar for the entire duration of this earthly experience that we call human life. This vehicle allows you to travel, experience emotions, experience pleasure, and do all of the things that bodies do. And that body has a computer—your mind. You are the being, the soul, that sits behind that computer and uses it to operate the body to move through the world. But the mind is not who you are. And even though you look out of your body's eyes, the body is not who you are either.

You are something deep and universal and ancient that sits at the core of your very being. And you can practice watching your life pass in front of you, kind of like watching a movie, being a witness to it all. Not to detach but to shift your perspective and learn how to respond rather than react. Connect with that deep soul part of you. When you do, you'll learn to be the calmness below the surface waters. Up on the waves is the drama of everyday life, and rather than get swept up in all that drama, you can instead choose to notice how the drama and the story is not you and that these things cannot really touch you.

The fact that you are not your body or your feelings or anything else so simple means that when those things become "hurt," your true self does not also become hurt. You are a spiritual being, a vast light body of energy, and you're just being squeezed into a human body for the time being. And nothing— *nothing!*—here on this earthly plane can hurt the real you. It's like how when your avatar in a video game becomes injured, you don't feel the pain. You are here gathering experiences, and even though things might feel so big and important or like the end of the world when they happen, when you go back to the spirit plane after you transition through death, you're able to look at events rather objectively. There won't be any heightened emotions attached to experiences, no lens which to view them through, and you'll see them for what they truly are, just events. Things that happened. Nothing more, nothing less. What you'll be more interested in, is if you grew from them.

There's a beautiful quote by the Sufi poet Rumi that I love that goes: "This place is a dream. Only a sleeper considers it real.

Then death comes like dawn and you wake up laughing at what you thought was your grief."[2]

So things that happen here are stories and opportunities to learn and grow and that's it. The world doesn't get to experience your gifts if you're just beating yourself up or wallowing in sadness or anger or resentment. That is not why you, a multi-dimensional being full of infinite powers, incarnated into this life.

What we really need to learn to do is to separate the real from our perceptions of what's real. And because we are existing inside of an illusion, a school, a play, most of what we believe is real with our minds is just us placing meaning on top of something where no meaning once was.

Forgive Yourself Too

While you are going around forgiving everyone else in your life, don't forget to forgive yourself too. You are an actor as well, and you played a part too. Perhaps you even inadvertently caused someone else to hurt. You might have had wonderful intentions that were misunderstood by someone. Maybe you made a mistake but were doing the best you could with what you had at the time, or maybe you were lashing out because you had a bad day. Whatever the reason, it still doesn't matter because things are only as good or bad as you decide they are. And, of course, as the other person decides they are, but how they interpret your actions and words is entirely on them. You are only responsible for your interpretation, reaction, and response while they are responsible for theirs.

---

2   *The Essential Rumi*, trans. Coleman Barks with John Moyne (New York: Harper San Francisco, 1995)

We are so good at judging ourselves and beating ourselves up. If we make a mistake, it can make us feel stupid, unworthy, embarrassed, and completely strip us of our confidence. You need to let go of any guilt you might be carrying.

Guilt is a low-frequency vibration. It's punishing yourself before anyone else has a chance to. When we do something we think is bad, we expect to be berated or punished by our parents, our teachers, our bosses, God, or anyone else. So we feel guilty as a way to hurt ourselves in payment for this wrongdoing.

But you're doing it all to yourself. When you really look at the situation, more often than not you'll find that you're punishing yourself because of inexperience, lack of education, innocence, or that you simply didn't know any better at the time.

We can hold onto pain for so long—months, years, decades, even a lifetime. It satiates a part of us that is subconsciously trying to get rid of our guilt through self-punishment. We think we deserve to feel miserable, so we make ourselves feel that way. But eventually you need to get conscious and ask yourself how long this is going to go on. How much guilt is enough? How much blame is enough? How much of your happiness and your life do you need to sacrifice to repay this perceived debt? Or these perceived wrongdoings, whether they're real or completely made up? If there is some amount of time where you feel like you've officially paid your debt, like you can finally let it go, then why not have that amount of time be "right away?"

Instead of spending your time thinking about how you are guilty or bad or a terrible person, think about examples of how you are innocent, wonderful, and perfect exactly as you are. You have become an expert in coming up with reasons why you are guilty and should feel shame and humiliation. Use that same skill to come up with reasons for why you are innocent. It's time to change your dialogue around it. Flip the script. If you're feeling stuck, ask a coach or a good friend whom you trust to help you. I do this often in my life-coaching practice with my private clients. Sometimes we're so deep in this self-deprecating mindset that we can't see things beyond our limited point of view. Rewrite your story and change your mind so that you can let go of toxic emotions weighing you down that will ultimately harm you. And then, stop thinking about the event altogether! Stop replaying scenarios over and over in your mind, stop obsessing about the details, stop thinking about what you should have done or said. All this does is torment your present moment.

Now ego might jump in and say you are lying to yourself, but remember things that happen to you, things other people say to you, things people do to you, and things you do to others are all neutral events. You place meaning on top of them by deciding that you are hurt or guilty, so you're technically lying to yourself when you decide these things as well. Either way, all you're doing is telling yourself a story you've made up. So now all you're doing by making the choice to see everything from a different perspective is reframing your story.

We all have been through all kinds of experiences. What we choose to focus on is what will create our present moment. So often, our mind is preoccupied with thinking about the past or the future, and because our thoughts are on the past or the future, we miss the present moment, which is the only true time there is. Because of this, we don't really understand time. So many of the great mystics and teachers out there, as well as A Course In

Miracles and Dolores's hypnosis subjects, tell us that time isn't linear, that we only perceive it on 3D Earth. Past lives are actually parallel lives. Those who have had near-death experiences where they crossed the veil have even reported seeing themselves living many time lines at once. Sometimes we get glimpses into this state of being outside of time when we are totally in the present moment. Have you ever been deep in meditation or in a flow state where you completely stopped experiencing time? This is the true nature of time – that there is only one time and that it is all happening simultaneously. We are living in a constant present moment, an eternal now.

Since the present moment is the only true time there is, whenever we think about the past we're telling stories and projecting illusions. If we choose to focus on painful memories, our story about the past becomes one of pain and we start to see the present moment through that same lens. When we focus on happy memories, our story about the past becomes happy, and we bring that same feeling and lens into the present moment. That's not to say that you should deny that something happened. You can instead flip your perspective—change your mind—about how you look at that thing that happened and how it affects you. Decide to see the positives that came out of it rather than dwell on what you perceive as negative.

Whether or not you buy into the idea that time isn't linear, one fact remains true. The past is over. It can only influence your present moment if you allow it to. You can choose to either forgive, forget, and heal, or to keep focusing on things that make you feel tormented. Both take the same amount of time and energy. In this way, your present can change your past. By remembering your past in a positive light, you change your story around it. If you remember back to the delayed-choice experiment in quantum physics, what we do in the present *can* alter our past.

Everyone is responsible for their own self, and if someone else perceived what you did as good or bad then that is because they are viewing the world through the lens that they have created based on their accumulated experiences and their thoughts about the world and themselves. But let go of the idea that you've done bad things because you haven't. You're an energetic light being here in a school having experiences for the purpose of learning lessons so that your soul can keep growing and expanding to newer and higher levels of consciousness. That's it.

All you can do is your best and be kind and don't purposefully cause anyone harm. If you make a mistake, learn from it and do better next time. Take the lesson and then leave behind the emotions associated with it. We're meant to learn lessons in this school, not endlessly punish ourselves.

You wouldn't punish a child forever for doing something wrong before they had all of the knowledge to make a better choice, so why doesn't the same apply to you?

Remember, ego loves duality and sees things in black and white. The way out of this vicious cycle of earthly duality is to rise above it and forgive and forget. The paradox is that you only need to forgive someone if you place blame on them. If you decide to withdraw that blame, if you change your mind and decide you don't need to assign good or bad to certain events, there will be nothing that even needs to be forgiven in the first place. All there is to do is forget and let things go.

What About People Who Have Done Bad Things?

The natural progression of thought at this point for the ego is to say something like, "Okay, I get the point you're making when it comes to mistakes or ways that we might have accidentally hurt someone else, but what about murderers and rapists and other criminals who intentionally do terrible things?"

I want to be clear that the change of mindset we're exploring is not about excusing anyone's behaviors. It is also not about giving free rein for people to go around creating havoc and committing crimes. Nor is it saying that you can or should treat people poorly. It is merely reframing your perspective on the perceived wrongdoings of yourself and the people in your life to allow you to forgive and release your anger, your hurt, your resentment, your guilt, and your sadness so you can then heal and flourish and live up to your fullest potential. If your lens is one of anger, then that is how you will interpret events around you, how you'll interact with others, what you'll project out into the world, and that anger will eat away at you, causing you harm, possibly eventually in the form of disease. It is poison, and holding onto poison only causes *you* harm.

When you operate from a place of anger, pain, revenge, and other low-vibration emotions, you might think you are doing good—most humans have good intentions, don't have the intention of causing others harm—but you can only cause more destruction and the cycle of pain continues. It's inevitable. The old adage "hurt people hurt people and healed people heal people" has a lot of truth to it. Remember that these are soul lessons you're accumulating here and you want to release these lower vibration emotions and let go of toxicity. Forgiveness is one of the truest and quickest paths there.

Now some people do horrendous things, that is true. One of my favorite quotes from *A Course in Miracles* goes: "Every act is either an expression of love or a call for love."[3] Read that again. "Every act is either an expression of love or a call for love." I think about this quote often as I go through life. Anytime someone offends me or lashes out at me, I often give pause and consider it. It can truly change the way you view the world and make you look upon others with compassion and empathy.

So am I saying that no one should ever go to prison? That people should be allowed to commit egregious acts like rape and murder? Definitely not. But people who commit these types of acts are hurting, deeply and badly. The only reason someone is able to find something outside of themselves to fight or hurt is because there is conflict and pain inside of them. When a person feels inner peace and love, they can only project peace and love onto the world. Alan Cohen compassionately reminds us in *A Course In Miracles Made Easy* that people who hurt others feel lost, helpless, lonely, confused, frustrated, and full of self-hatred. They have come untethered from love, from Source, and from their true Self. And by acting out on the pain festering inside of them, they are only bringing more of this energy back into their own lives. They are stuck in a cycle of destruction and pain. While it's important to get them off the streets until they are mentally and emotionally healthy so they do not hurt anyone else, it's also important to help them heal. When we help them heal, we

---

3   Scribed by Dr. Helen Schucman, *A Course in Miracles: Text, Vol. 1* (Foundation for Inner Peace, July 25, 2012)

fix the root problem rather than just place a bandage over the symptoms by locking them away. In the long run, healing will do a lot more than punishment ever could.

There's an amazing tradition of the people of the Babemba tribe in Africa. Any time a member of the tribe acts in a way that is harmful or does something "bad," they are brought into the middle of their village. All of the members of the tribe stop working and form a circle around them. Then, one by one, each member of the tribe tells something positive about the accused. They might tell a story about something great they have done, or talk about all of their positive character traits, or any skills they have, or any acts of kindness they have shown, and so on. They talk about what they love about them, their favorite memories with them. They recite these positive things in all of the detail they can remember and really take their time, making sure that the person hears their words. The ceremony can last for days. At the end, the tribe celebrates and symbolically welcomes the accused back into the tribe.

People that do horrific things are calling out for love. Chances are those people received very little love while they were growing up. If we respond with hate and turn away from them with coldness, we are reinforcing to them that the world is a cold, cruel, dark, and terrible place. If we bathe them in love, compassion, understanding, and forgiveness, we teach them a new lesson about the world. We change their mind and set the chain of events in motion that could ultimately lead to their healing. And who knows, maybe once they are healed they can bring great gifts to the world. This is the way we heal not only an individual person but also a sick society. Love is the ultimate healing tool.

We are all connected and what one person does affects us all. In quantum physics, this is called entanglement. It doesn't matter how far away particles are, when they are entangled, they remain linked. There's a famous physics experiment where scientists entangled two photons and then sent them off in opposing directions. Once the photons were a great distance apart, the scientists measured things like their position, momentum, and spin. They found that when they measured one of the entangled photons, there was a direct correlation with the second photon. Whenever something was observed happening to one of the photons, at the exact same moment, not a millisecond later, the second photon was affected as well. There was no time for the photons to communicate with one another, it was instantaneous. The two separated photons acted as though they were one single entity. Not only did this experiment blow Einstein's Theory of Relativity out of the water, but it proved that everything in our universe is connected.

Ken Keyes, Jr. wrote the book *The Hundredth Monkey* about a phenomenon that's come to be known as The Hundredth Monkey Effect. It started when scientists conducted a 30-year research project on the island of Koshima, Japan in which they studied a wild colony of *Macaca fuscata* monkeys. The scientists provided the monkeys with sweet potatoes, which they dropped in the sand. The monkeys loved the potatoes; not so much the sand that covered them. In 1952, a young monkey in the group started washing the sand off her potatoes in water. Soon, other monkeys in her family began to imitate this behavior, until practically every monkey on the island was doing it. Once a certain amount of monkeys were regularly washing their potatoes, a tipping point was reached and monkeys on other islands as well as mainland Japan all started washing their food the same way, even though they weren't physically witnessing the behavior taking place. It's like the information had uploaded into the collective consciousness of the breed.

In *The Ancient Secret of the Flower of Life,* Drunvalo Melchizedek explains this phenomenon by saying that each species on the planet has a special grid around the Earth that connects every single member of the species to one another.

Gregg Braden talks in his book *The Divine Matrix* about something similar: how there is a "cosmic canvas" that encompasses and intertwines all living things in our universe. It's impossible for someone to pull on one side of this canvas without it creating a reaction farther down on the canvas. Our actions send out ripple effects everywhere.

Still others call this the quantum field, the unified field of consciousness, or the great hologram. Whatever you like to call it, one truth remains: we are all connected. It is in every one's best interest to help those who are suffering.

Anita Moorjani had a near-death experience (NDE) where she crossed over to the other side of the veil after battling terminal cancer for four years and slipping into a coma when her organs shut down. While on the other side, she found herself surrounded by unconditional love and absolutely no judgment whatsoever. She describes in her book *Dying to Be Me* how this experience shaped her life once she came back fully healed with no trace of cancer by saying that she lost the ability to judge and discern good from bad, right from wrong. She had experienced such a profound state of unconditional love and wasn't judged for a single thing she had done in her life during her NDE and she brought that state of awareness back with her. She found herself with only compassion for criminals and terrorists as well as their victims because she saw that they were coming from a place of deep inner pain. She commented on how they were emotionally diseased, similar to how she had been physically diseased with cancer. She stopped seeing the world in terms of victims and perpetrators because she had felt with such certainty that we are all one. We're all creating society together through our actions, thoughts, and beliefs.

"Good" people do bad things and "bad" people do good things, and no one is inherently one or the other. No one is good or evil. In the end, it is that person's soul lessons or karma to work out. And by karma I don't mean that they should get their legs broken in this lifetime. I mean that in their next lifetime they will be born into circumstances that will help them overcome any lesson they didn't learn in this one. The universe has a way of balancing things out, but it's not about punishment. For those stuck in a repetitive cycle of the abused victim who abuses and victimizes, their lesson first and foremost has to be how to break this cycle and heal. In the meantime, we human beings can work on our compassion and capacity to love and forgive to help ease our own karma and propel our own growth forward. It's easy to feel love for people who do good things, but it's much more difficult to feel love for the people who really need it.

Can you imagine how the world would change if we all put this into practice like the Babemba tribe does?

There was an experiment done in Washington, D.C. in 1993, the crime capital of the US at the time, where hundreds of people came to the city and sat in meditation and sent out thoughts of peace for two months. Before the experiment, violent crimes like rapes and homicides had been steadily increasing. When they measured the crime rate after the mass meditation, it had fallen substantially by 25 percent. Not only that, but there were less car accidents and emergency room visits during that time period as well.

A multitude of similar experiments have taken place in prisons, cities, and schools throughout the world with the same results, including in war-torn areas in the Middle East. After a while, researchers were able to get such good data that they could actually pinpoint the exact percentage of a population who needs to meditate on peace in order for a tipping point to be reached and for a change to occur. The magic number is the square root of 1 percent of a city's (or school's, prison's, country's, region's, etc.) population. This is the number needed just to create minimal change. For the world's population, that means less than 9,000 people. Imagine what would happen if a larger percentage of the population meditated on peace in this same way. Reality truly is affected by the thoughts, energy, and emotions we put out and we do live in a holographic universe, with each piece affecting the whole.

Rather than focusing on condemning others, if we instead work on our own healing, our own inner peace, and our own capacity to love, we would reflect those qualities out into the world and the world would rise to meet our new level of consciousness. Don't wait for someone else to go first. Rise first and then offer others a hand to help lift everyone else up to a higher level.

How Do We Cope with the Idea that We Create Our Reality?

Sometimes hearing that you create your own reality is a tough pill to swallow. Some people balk at the idea that they create their own reality and that they chose the circumstances they are born into. They look around and say, "But there is racism, sexism, government control, inequalities of all kinds, squalid living conditions for some people, homelessness, disease, poverty, and history is filled with genocides and wars." They think about the traumas of their own life and those of their ancestral line. Everyone has a story, and every family tree has a story too. My father's side of the family is Jewish, and I myself have many, many relatives who were slaughtered during the Holocaust.

Remember, we are powerful beings from the stars incarnated here and we are all one and we are all connected. We've forgotten our true spiritual nature and believe that what we're experiencing right here, right now on Earth is real and is all there is. All of these things are man-made concepts, the stage set of a play, the setting of a movie. None of these societal rules are real. They are just something we have all agreed to, an illusion that we have collectively come to believe is real.

In Hinduism, they call the world "Maya," which means "illusion." Because they knew that our world is a projection, a dream, a veil lowered before our eyes like a filter. "Māyā is the empirical reality that entangles consciousness. Māyā has the power to create a bondage to the empirical world, preventing the unveiling of the true, unitary self—the Cosmic Spirit..."[4] ISKON

4   Alex Dopico, "What is maya in Indian philosophy?" (janetpanic.com, August 7, 2020)

Education Services explains it well: "Under Māyā's influence, the *atman*, (the soul) mistakenly identifies with the body. He accepts such thoughts as 'I am white and I am a man,' or 'This is my house, my country, and my religion.' Thus the illusioned soul identifies with the temporary body and everything connected to it, such as race, gender, family, nation, bank balance, and sectarian religion."[5]

The Four Agreements talks about how we get so attached to this illusion. And we've appointed ourselves both judge and victim. Ego thrives on drama, fear, suffering, and negative emotions. Since we believe that our ego is who we are, we get so attached to being the judge and the victim and it's difficult to shed these beliefs. We even get so comfortable with suffering that it makes us feel safe. But judgment is a man-made concept. Remember, you are a part of Source. And there is no judgment there. You are loved unconditionally simply for being, for existing.

You can look out into the world and find a million excuses to be angry, to cast blame, to feel like a victim. If you're looking for something to fight, it's easy to find it. But you always have a choice.

I've also heard ego say things like, "It's easy to believe all of these things if you come from a place of privilege." The truth is this power is in all of us. No one race, social class, or nationality of people is more powerful or less powerful. All of these differences are superficial, the avatar that we chose.

---

5   Retrieved from: https://iskconeducationalservices.org/HoH/concepts/key-concepts/maya-illusion/

Quantum Physics as well as a multitude of ancient cultures and texts from around the globe all tell us that we are all connected by an invisible energy field and what someone does on one side of the planet greatly affects what someone else does on the other side of it. Everyone affects the world and other people. Reality is like a hologram in that each tiny piece reflects the entire whole and we are projecting reality out from our inner worlds into this energy field. If you know anything about how a hologram works, you know that you can cut it up into as many pieces of various sizes as you'd like, and inside of each piece you'll still see a reflection of the entire image. So if you are thinking thoughts of duality, of separateness, of "us" versus "them," then you are helping to call that paradigm into existence.

Have you ever thought about someone and then they call you the next day or you run into them? For me, it happens often with dreams. I'll dream about someone I haven't thought about or seen in a long time, and then the next day I'll find out some big piece of news about them - they got married or had a baby or some other big life event—or they'll come back into my life after a long hiatus.

My friends jokingly call me an alien because of these strange occurrences that happen to me, and my husband tells me I have magical powers. The truth though is that we are all capable of this because we are all connected. There is an invisible field, a tapestry, that runs through and envelops all of life, binding us all together and weaving our lives inextricably like dazzling threads.

There is so much more going on than we realize, and the universe and life is so much bigger and more complex and fascinating than the petty problems we find ourselves indulging in here on planet Earth. I personally find it so hard to understand why the majority of humanity is focused on and gets so emotional about such small and fleeting drama rather than asking and thinking and talking about bigger and more mind-expanding topics like the universe and life.

We all have the ability to change our thoughts and beliefs and thus change our reality. My hope is that this book and these teachings empower everyone. We need to work to bring humanity together so that we can collectively raise the consciousness of the planet, rather than find reasons to further divide it.

The best way for you to know if this works is to try it. Think your own thoughts rather than allowing all of these outside influences to tell you what you should be thinking. My job isn't to force you to change or even to make you believe everything that I am saying. I'm just here to offer another perspective, to show you that there is another way of thinking and being in our world. You have your own free will. You can choose to take what resonates and leave what doesn't. You can choose to try the things that I'm sharing and see if they work for you or to dismiss them without trying them.

A lot of times because of fear, we tend to dismiss new ideas quickly. And because we're scared we don't want to try new things so we make up reasons to convince ourselves why they won't work—we try to validate our fear. This is all the work of the ego. Remember ego can be the voice of the cynic, the realist. It wants to keep you safe. And sometimes the idea that you are powerful and that you create your own reality is absolutely terrifying to the ego.

Remember, ego will make up any reason and tell you any story to convince you of why you can't have what you want. Instead, be more interested in the life you're manifesting than the part of you that tries to convince you you can't have that thing.

Julia Cannon and Kaya Wittenburg responded to this so elegantly in a webinar they hosted on the Dolores Cannon Facebook page. They essentially said that there are always different realities and worlds constantly going on at the same time. All you have to do to see this is look at two opposing groups who strongly believe their way is the right way to feel like they're living in different worlds. If you can imagine another reality, it exists. Since thousands of possible realities exist and nothing is concrete, any one of them can be correct and you can call into your existence whichever one you'd like. So focus your energy on the world you want to create. Calibrate yourself with whichever reality you want. The choice is yours. If you can visualize it, feel it, see yourself inside of it, and your thoughts and beliefs align with it, then that reality will become yours.

The more you focus on what you want, the more the world handed to you by default will start to fade away and the reality you want will come into clearer focus. It's alchemy: you're transforming darkness into light, stress into peace of mind, anger into joy.

If you look around and see a pained, sick, and tormented world, by thinking that you're going to make it so. Whatever you get emotional about is what you'll get more of. Remember, feeling emotions is how we tune ourselves to specific frequencies and how we choose specific realities from the quantum realm. So by getting emotional about a situation, you're aligning yourself with it. It's like the Facebook algorithm—whatever you interact with, the universe thinks you like and will send you more of. But life isn't happening to you. You are doing it. You're causing it to happen. You have to completely switch around the way you look at reality. The outside world isn't happening regardless of what happens with you; the outside world is a projection of your thoughts, like a movie playing in real time all around you that you control. You're not a victim of society, oppression, or other people. You are a creator. You attract what you believe to be true about the world. So change your mind and see a new reality instead. You have an infinite number of options.

Here's another thing to consider: If you do research looking for something to support your beliefs, you're sure to find something that does. Think again about any two opposing groups in the world that you know of—each one adamantly and unwaveringly believes that they are right and they can back it up with all sorts of data and figures and writings and experts that they've found. People can be living next door to each other and seem to be living in two different worlds. There's always going to be information out there from every viewpoint possible, and most of that information consists of opinions and perspectives, not facts and truths. At the end of the day, you get to make a choice about what you look at. Each choice you make will bring into fruition a different reality. Focus on what you want rather than what you don't want. Cut out everything that doesn't support the reality you want, give zero of your attention and energy to it. If the news is talking about something like unemployment or a real estate crash that's affecting your area, you can simply affirm, "This does not affect me."

When you think in this way you are taking the power away from outside forces and putting it back into your own hands. By knowing that you create your own reality, you can feel empowered rather than defensive because you get to create whatever you want.

CHAPTER 7

CLEARING NEGATIVITY OUT OF YOUR LIFE

Have you ever held a newborn baby? Looked into their eyes and just saw innocence and wonder? Did you ever meet a baby you thought wasn't worthy? Of course not! Babies are fresh from the universe.

So why do you believe *you* are unworthy? You came into this world the same way as that baby, innocent and full of wonder. So what happened? Why did you start to have doubts somewhere along the way and decide you are not worthy?

When we were kids, we used to run around and express our emotions freely and be 100% ourselves. We didn't try to change for anybody. We didn't think badly about ourselves. We just were in the present moment. If we were sad, we cried. If we were frustrated, maybe we threw a tantrum. If we were joyful, we laughed. If we had energy, we ran around. If we were excited, we raised our voice emphatically. This is our natural state, where our emotions flow freely and we are completely in the present moment.

But then something happened. Our parents started telling us things like "Stop screaming, you can't do that in public," or "No running around in the store," or "Stop yelling in the house." If we were bad, then we got punished, either yelled at or worse. If we were quiet and good and just sat there and followed the old "children are meant to be seen, not heard" cliche, then we were told we were good and got rewarded. Our teachers started to tell us the same things. In fact, all of the adults started doing this. And pretty soon we came to believe that we are not perfect and the way we behave is bad. At our core, all human beings want to be loved. When we are rewarded, we feel loved. When we are punished, we fear that we are not loved. So we learned to hold our emotions inside. We curbed our personalities to conform to this idea of society. And we did that by holding our breath. It was the only way we knew how to push those emotions deep down inside and keep them there so we could behave as expected.

Have you ever watched a baby breathe? They breathe deep into their bellies. This is the natural way of breathing. It's how humans are supposed to breathe. It increases the supply of oxygen and nutrients to the entire body, relaxes muscles and relieves tension, supports muscle growth and provides energy, keeps blood pressure low, and a whole host of other things. When we belly breathe and allow our emotions to flow freely, we are relaxed and in the flow of life.

When we started unconsciously holding our emotions inside, we were feeling all of that tension and the only way to lock it away was to change our breathing patterns, so most adults breathe with their upper chest area only. You can test it out by lying down on your back and placing one hand on your belly and one on your chest and just breathe normally without trying to control it. Chances are, the hand on your chest will rise and fall much more than the hand on your belly. We literally rewired our bodies to respond to the tension we were feeling in our minds. And by constricting our breathing up into our chest, we're holding tension inside of our bodies and thus not allowing ourselves to live up to our true potential.

Place your hands out in front of you with your palms touching, the right hand on top, palm facedown and the left hand underneath, palm faceup. Now press your hands against each other with all of your strength. The left hand with palm facing up is all of your repressed emotions trying to break free. Your right hand with palm facing down is you keeping your emotions shoved down. Now just look at how much energy you're expending keeping all of that junk locked in place. Now, very quickly while still applying pressure, take your right hand off. What happens? Your left hand flies up, and all of the metaphorical repressed emotions explode out because the pressure has been released.

Emotions are energy and can be powerful, and when we push them down, they don't have anywhere else to go but into our body where they get stuck and become repressed emotions. And this energy doesn't just disappear. It stays there, blocking the natural flow of energy in our bodies, causing our muscles to tense up, and either turns into pain, disease (dis-ease), or bubbles up to the surface at inappropriate times and in inappropriate ways.

If we could learn to release this tension, we could heal so much. If we could learn to be in the flow of life, we could access those deeper parts of ourselves. But because we've been holding those emotions in for so long and it's turned into tensions in our bodies and affected the way we breathe and move through the world for so long, it's become an unconscious program, habit, and pattern that we need to consciously unwind.

Releasing Toxic Emotions with Grace

When you keep repressing emotions, eventually you're going to exhaust yourself from trying to keep them down. It's not sustainable. You'll either run yourself ragged and make yourself sick or your rage and anger and sadness will get unleashed out into the world, oftentimes directed at someone you project negativity onto and sometimes even at those you love. When we learn to allow our emotions to flow freely rather than drive them down, we don't have to use this extra energy to keep them in place. Imagine what you could do with that extra energy, like use it to heal, to create, to live fully.

We're here to have experiences as human beings and that means feeling the whole range of emotions that is available to us—from the heartbreaking that brings you to your knees to the boundless joy that makes you throw your arms wide open to everything in between. The problem happens when we hide our shame, shove down our anger, or deny our grief, which essentially allows these emotions to unconsciously control our life. Emotions are meant to be felt and then released, but in our modern society, we have a tendency to push them down rather than allow ourselves to fully feel them. Maybe we're in a hurry during our busy day and someone says something at work that hurts, so we swallow down the lump in our throat and force ourselves to push forward. Sometimes we more purposely escape what we're feeling. We want to stay unconscious and avoid our feelings, so we do anything to keep ourselves from confronting them, like watch TV, constantly have to be around people socializing, spend alone time looking at social media or texting others, listen to music, dive into work, travel, shop, eat, drink, exercise, have sex, look at dating apps, and play video games. Even when we are doing something we enjoy, like attending a concert or going on a hike, we take pictures of it to share rather than just being in the present moment and enjoying it. We do anything to numb our minds so that we can distract ourselves and avoid doing the inner work.

One of the best things we can do to heal is allow ourselves to fully feel our emotions so that they can then dissipate. And it doesn't take long. It can take mere moments. Once you allow yourself to feel a repressed emotion, it will quickly morph into another emotion. Oftentimes anger will morph into sadness, for example, because the real emotion at the root is sadness, but our ego has turned it into anger as a way to protect us. The emotions will continue to morph as you release them until finally they completely dissipate and you don't have to carry them around with you anymore.

Fear is a big emotion that we all deal with. When we take a step back and really look at our fears, we can see that most of what we fear isn't actually happening.

A good friend who has been in the AA world for many decades taught me that fear is an acronym for "False Evidence Appearing

Real." She also taught me this exercise for releasing fears. This is where that list you made of all of your fearful thoughts comes in. You can use the list as a jumping off point if you don't know where to start or nothing comes to mind. At the top of a piece of paper write:

"I am resentful that/at _____ because I have fear that: _____."

Then choose one thing you are resentful at and fill in the first blank. Let's say you choose to write in "my partner." Then start listing all of your fears related to your partner. Let them just flow out stream-of-consciousness style onto the paper, one after the other. Keep writing anything that pops into your head. Don't think about what you're writing and don't judge or try to analyze it. Just keep going. Don't hold back. Let pen fly to paper. Don't stop moving your pen. You'll find that one fear will lead to another, like peeling away the layers of an onion, and pretty soon you'll find that your fear, at its very core, had nothing to do with your partner at all. So for example, maybe your list looks like this:

He'll break up with me.

I'll end up alone.

I'm not good enough.

My parents think I'm not good enough too.

I'm not a good daughter.

I'm scared of losing my mother.

More often than not when I do this, fears get uncovered that were lurking deep in my subconscious, well below the surface. After you've exhausted all of your fears and feel you've expelled them all, look at your lists—both the one you've been keeping in your journal and the one you just created—and ask yourself these two questions:

1. Is any of this happening right now?
2. Is any of this something I want to happen?

After seeing that the answer to both questions will likely be resounding no's, tell your lists of fears, "None of this is going to happen, and even if it does, I'll use the experience to learn and grow." Then rip up the pieces of paper and throw them out, burn them, shred them, delete them if they're digital, whatever you need to do to clear them away. This symbolically releases your fears and also keeps them from manifesting.

You can do this exercise with anything—your job, the government, sexism, your finances, a person in your life, a situation you're in. And you can do it as many times as you need to. I recommend doing it once a week to keep clearing out fearful thoughts.

A lot of people who are into manifesting and journaling are scared to write down their fears because they think they'll come true if they put pen to paper similar to how their Manifest Memoir does. But that's not the case. For starters, in the Manifest Memoir we are using very specific language. This fear exercise accomplishes a few very powerful things. First, it clears these fears out of your mind. You pull the thoughts out and physically throw them away and then they aren't circulating around in your head anymore. Remember, it's the thoughts you think that are the seeds that grow into your beliefs and manifestations. Not releasing them means they are going to seep into manifesting and create your reality. Another thing it does is force you to see that your fear often stems from something much deeper, not the thing on the surface you're actually worrying about. And finally, looking at your fears and seeing them for what they are—simply ideas about a possible future that hasn't happened—takes away their power. You are able to look at everything and logically understand that none of these things are happening right now while affirming to yourself that even if they did, you'd be okay.

This human experience can be so beautiful. Allow yourself to fully feel it all. Feel everything, live into the moment, unapologetically embrace your humanness. But then let those emotions go with grace.

Triggers Are Mirrors

As you're exploring this realm of toxic emotions and learning to release them, another important thing to pay attention to is what triggers you. Triggers are mirrors that reveal what we are still working through by showing us what we find upsetting about the outside world or another person. Anything you get emotional about, that triggers you, is showing you the parts of yourself that are unhealed. If you had already healed from a specific issue, you wouldn't have such a highly charged emotional reaction when it is reflected back to you. People who can find offense in pretty much anything another person says or does have a lot of healing to do. When you are healed, you understand that what others say and do has absolutely nothing to do with you.

So pay attention to what triggers you and use those as clues to look deep inside. I recommend writing down triggers as they come up so you can start to do some deep work about why that person or situation or thing brought about such an emotional reaction. Once you start to understand the what, you can begin uncovering the why, and that is when true healing happens. Because remember, events and things that people say or do are neutral. It is you placing meaning and emotion on top of them that makes them good or bad, triggering or unimportant. The eventual goal is to be able to take a step back, view events objectively, and thoughtfully respond rather than emotionally react. Or, if you really become masterful, to just let them go completely without even having to respond.

When we really take the time to look at what is making us feel angry, upset, frustrated, or resentful, we often uncover that it's not the event or person we originally thought it was. We are rarely upset for the reason we think we are. Events and things that people say don't make you angry or upset. You are already angry and upset, and the events and people give you excuses to unleash those feelings out into the wild.

Hawkins explains it so well in *Letting Go: The Pathway of Surrender*. He says that people with repressed emotions are like pressure-cookers just waiting to release steam any chance they can get. They blame outside forces for upsetting them, but really, their repressed emotions are always looking for an excuse to vent themselves. Psychiatrists call this displacement. The only reason events and people make us angry is because we already are angry.

Getting triggered and upset uses up so much of your precious energy because you get so wrapped up in anger and anxiety and placing blame and playing the victim. All of that energy would be much better used on your own self-healing and development, spending time doing things that bring you joy with people you love, and giving your gifts to the world. Rather than focusing on what everyone else is or isn't doing or is or isn't saying, focus on *your* purpose. Everything else is just a distraction.

People who trigger you are especially interesting. Everyone you meet is a mirror for you. It's impossible to love or hate something about someone else unless you love or hate that exact same thing in yourself.

Since we are all pieces of the same, everyone you meet is also a reflection of your thoughts and how you think about the world. Through this lens, you are manifesting how that person will act toward you. If you expect or perceive someone will be rude and standoffish, then that is the way they are going to act. If you expect or perceive them to be warm and friendly, then that is the way they are going to act. People show up the way you see them or expect them to. And there's a pretty good chance that the way *they* perceive *you* is the same way you are perceiving them.

Back in college, a friend of mine once told me about a girl in her class who was a super tough egg to crack. "I tried to be friendly to her and make her feel comfortable, but she's always so cold, unfriendly, and aloof toward me," my friend vented one night. They had several mutual friends, and everyone told her the other girl was cool and nice. My friend couldn't figure it out. "It feels like she's two different people. She likes and is nice to everyone else, but she has a million walls up toward me."

Finally, months later after spending more forced time around each other due to mutual friends, they grew on each other and had a chance to talk and connect one-on-one. I remember my friend recounting the conversation to me. "She admitted to me that she saw me as being cold, unfriendly, and aloof toward her. I was absolutely stunned. She used the exact same words to describe me as I had used to describe her!"

Of course, my initial reaction was surprise. My friend was incredibly generous and welcoming and loved bringing people together. "How can anyone think that about you? You're so loving and friendly?!" I questioned.

But then I paused. In that moment I realized that's exactly how I viewed my friend, so that's exactly how she was to me. Those were the qualities I chose to focus on. That was the lens I had of her.

This situation with my friend wasn't an isolated incident. I started noticing this occurring in my own life once I had this new perspective and awareness. Any time someone has told me honestly what they think of me, I've been shocked to find out it was the exact same way I've thought of them, down to the same descriptive words.

We make split-second judgments on people when we meet them. Within the first few seconds, we subconsciously decide if we like someone or not based on our lens. When we look out into the world and expect people to behave a certain way or make a snap judgment about someone's personality, then exactly what we believe will come true.

Everyone is a reflection of you. People and the outside world appear to be separate from ourselves, but the reality we see is merely a projection of our thoughts. If you think a person is unkind or a situation is cruel, you have a raging battle inside that you merely project onto the outer world. When life is treating you well and you're feeling kindness and love because you're happy, you project those same qualities out onto the world.

Choose Kindness Over Cancel Culture

There's a phenomenon sweeping the nation right now called "cancel culture," where whole groups of people become triggered and then lash out at a specific target over social media from the safe anonymity of behind their computer screens. Even more wild is that others will often jump on board the band wagon who weren't even triggered just because they were influenced by the thought-form of energy the group has created.

A thought-form of energy occurs when multiple people start thinking the same way about something. The energy of the emotion they put into that thing starts to take on a life of its own. Momentum builds, gathering more people in its wake, until it becomes difficult for people to escape this hive mind, ask a different question, think for themselves, and make a new choice.

Cancel culture is essentially a group of people choosing to have an emotional reaction where they might instead choose to have an empathetic conversation. They're missing out on the opportunity to cultivate true understanding, compassion, and healing. But they are mis-stepping because the way we start to heal the rest of the world is by first healing ourselves. They're appointing themselves as judge and placing blame on another rather than expanding into a higher version of themselves and helping to lift up humanity.

We're all here learning and growing, and we're all pieces of the same and reflections of each other. A person can't help heal society by stepping on another person or kicking them when they're down. The sadness, shame, anger, and other emotions you make others feel when you target them is sent off into the world and then the world gets more events that make people feel this way.

It's like creating a war so that you can fight for peace. We are not individuals. People and things out in the world appear separate from us but this is part of the illusion. We are all connected. The world is a hologram, with each tiny piece reflecting the whole. What happens to one of us happens to us all. You can't fight the outside world without fighting yourself; you can't heal the outside until you first heal yourself.

It's time to choose kindness no matter what anyone else chooses. It's time to step into a place of unconditional love and acceptance for our fellow humans. The way we heal society is through compassion and love, not through division and hate. This human experience can be hard enough as it is. Let's not make the ride any more difficult for anyone else.

Connection Between Emotions, Pain, and Illness

Illness can be a sensitive topic because people can get so attached to their illnesses, which is mistake number one. Never claim an illness as yours and never say that you are sick. Always say that you are healing or recovering. The words you use matter!

Pain is an interesting thing. The science of pain tells us that pain originates not in the body part that hurts but in learned neural pathways in the brain and the nervous system. This is true for all types of pain you experience, from a broken arm to a backache to a migraine. When the nervous system takes on stress, it can reach a tipping point where it presents as pain. It is the body's way of telling us it's overloaded and saying, "No more!" After a while, these pain pathways become so much of a habit for the body, that it fires up pain at just the slightest little trigger. This is when pain becomes chronic. The good news is that just as your brain learned this behavior and response, it can unlearn it as well.

Let's look at a few different ideas around pain and illness.

In *A Course in Miracles Made Easy* Alan Cohen says that physical and emotional pain and illness is our way of holding someone else guilty for hurting us. Think of common phrases such as: You make me sick, you'll be the death of me, my kid is a pain in the neck, this project is a real headache, I can't stomach that coworker.

The *Mindbody Prescription* by John E. Sarno says pain is caused by repressed emotions, mostly unexpressed rage that you've been holding onto, which causes constricted blood vessels. Your body reacts in pain as a way to protect you from feeling the emotions instead.

SoulSpeak by Julia Cannon talks about how pain is your body trying to give you messages. In her book, she says pain on the right side of the body is related to something going on now, in the present. And pain on the left side relates to something that happened in the past. She gives examples, such as problems with the circulatory system are related to being in the flow of your life. Issues with your legs, feet, and ankles mean you're not physically moving in your desired direction. Issues with your arms mean you need to release and let go of something. Fluid and/or water retention can signify a buildup of emotions and that you're not letting your emotions out or letting them flow. And so on.

Dolores Cannon talks about how through her work she's found that a lot of cancer, especially colon cancer, is caused by suppressed anger. People can't talk about their emotions, so they just hold them inside. We all carry so much junk around inside of us and the colon holds a great deal of not only our physical waste, but our emotional waste as well. When it isn't released, it festers and starts to eat away at you and you become sick.

Anita Moorjani, who had a mind-shattering near-death experience she chronicled in her stunning book *Dying to Be Me*, believes that illness is your soul trying to give you a wake-up call.

The Curable app, a phone app for those who suffer from chronic pain, takes a more scientific approach when talking about pain, interviewing and quoting many influential Western doctors who treat chronic pain patients. They tell us that each person's nervous system produces and responds to pain in a unique way and this can change over time. Pain is a way for your brain to keep you safe and it uses your thoughts, fears, feelings, and other stress you experience to learn how to do this. The brain essentially gets set to an ultra-sensitive and overprotective setting in people who experience chronic pain, so those people get increased pain responses to stimuli that would be normal or mild for others. Doctors and researchers have seen this happening directly on brain imaging studies. People with chronic pain literally have changes in their brain structure and function. Their brains are telling them there is physical damage in the body even when there actually is not.

A lot of it comes down to your thoughts about pain. Let's say you have a back injury and moving makes you feel pain. You then start to fear that pain. This fear becomes amplified over time and you get stuck in a cycle. Your brain becomes more sensitive and hypervigilant and sends you more pain signals, and since you're always looking out for them, you notice them more—it feeds into each other. The other part of the problem is that when pain becomes chronic, we attend to it more. You start thinking about the pain more, you start talking about the pain more, you focus your attention on the pain more, and your feelings associated with it become increasingly negative. All this only serves to drive the fear associated with it.

Studies have shown that focusing on your pain in this way can make it much worse. The Curable app recommends consciously focusing your thoughts and attention on other things to unwind this cycle of tension. Instead of avoiding activities because of your pain, to go do them. Talk about something besides your pain. Many times, when you focus on something else, your brain suppresses the pain.

What I find especially interesting is that the Curable app talks about how the way you think and feel about pain specifically isn't the only thing that makes a difference—it's also your overall mindset and outlook on life that determines how likely it is that your pain will become chronic. People who have a strong internal locus of control, meaning they believe in their own ability to influence events and outcomes in their life, have less frequent and intense pain. This is so in-line with everything we've been discussing, that your beliefs and your lens shape the reality you live in. On the other hand, people with a strong external locus of control, those who think the outcomes in their life are a result of fate, luck, and the actions of others, are reported to have more frequent and intense pain.

Other personality traits such as perfectionism, bottling up emotions, and a strong inner critic also make people more susceptible to pain. Stress also greatly influences pain. It's common for serious pain conditions and disease to appear out of the blue or worsen around stressful life events.

The app goes on to assure readers with some good news that the brain and nervous system can always be reprogrammed. The Curable app finds that simply educating its users about how pain works can help minimize their pain.

In *The Mindbody Prescription*, John E. Sarno says that sometimes he simply has to explain the relationship of pain to repressed emotions in his seminars and a large majority of his audience's chronic pain will completely dissipate before he even gets to the exercises to help them.

One common thread seems to connect all of these viewpoints on pain and illness: they are very much tied to our thoughts and emotions. Your body shows you what thoughts you're thinking, how you feel about yourself and the world, and what emotions you're feeling. Pain and illness are our body trying to tell us that something is out of alignment. It's the way it talks to us. Usually by the time disease shows up, our body has been attempting to communicate to us for a long time. It's literally screaming at us to wake up and make a change.

In modern society, we use prescription drugs to mask the messages our body is sending to tell us something is wrong or in disharmony (our symptoms). It's much like your house being on fire and your smoke detector going off. You can take the batteries out of the smoke detector and it'll stop the noise, aka the symptom, but the root problem still remains.

This idea of pain starting in our mind might make some people bristle and think that I'm trying to say, "It's all in your head" or "You're making it up," but I'm not saying that at all.

On the contrary, I believe the pain you are feeling is very real and very valid. Because remember, whatever you decide in your mind becomes your reality. So it becomes just as real as anything possibly could. Pretty soon, this pain or illness becomes your story. It becomes the reason you aren't as active anymore, the reason you can't meet your friends for lunch, the reason you can't work anymore, the reason you do or don't do any particular thing in your life. It's the thing you love to talk about. It soon morphs into your identity. And then it becomes comfortable. People can become so identified with and comfortable with their pain or disease that they actually don't want to heal because their identity is so wrapped up in it and they don't even know who they are without it. And sometimes they get value out of staying sick or in pain.

Staying sick is a choice, just like healing is. Alan Cohen says in *A Course in Miracles Made Easy* that some people choose to stay sick because they believe they'll benefit from it. He points to common perceived payoffs to illness, such as not having to go to school or work or do things you don't want to do; getting attention and sympathy from others; getting money from the government; and being able to get revenge or to be 'right' by making someone else out to be wrong.

I used to get really bad tension headaches. They started while I was working at the tech industry start-up, and I thought it was because I sat at a computer all day. They were so debilitating. I would get them several times each month, and they would last for around five days at a time. Nothing would make them go away. I would get a chiropractic adjustment, acupuncture, and a type of physical therapy called Egoscue every week. I would take

Advil, use ice, and use heat, and all of that combined would *sort of* dull the pain enough to get me to a place where I could *kind of* function. It was awful. The various practitioners told me it was likely caused by clenching my jaw, which I would often do throughout the day without even realizing it. This went on for about seven years. When I left the tech industry to become a yoga teacher, the headaches improved but didn't completely go away. My theory of the computer turned into anytime I looked at my phone for too long. *It must be an ergonomic thing, or I clench my jaw when I look at it for too long*, I thought.

It wasn't until I had a QHHT session and had the practitioner ask my Higher Self while I was under hypnosis what was causing my headaches that I got a real answer. The answer I received was that they were caused by getting too wrapped up in the emotions of this planet and the human experience. I was told I needed to stop letting people and things get to me and focus more instead on my mission on this planet.

"Hmm," the practitioner replied. "I'm hearing that it's almost like there's so much emotion built up that there's pressure inside your head."

To me that translated to stress. I started thinking back to the time when the headaches first started. Within a month or two, Shane and I had gotten married, bought and moved into a new house, and started new jobs. They had all been positive things, but it had been a really stressful time. Then my next several jobs had all been high stress. I had started to believe that the headaches were triggered by sitting at a computer or staring at my phone for a long period of time, so whenever I did those things, a headache would pop up. It was such an ah-ha moment!

Since then, I've started paying attention to when headaches surface. They're always seemingly out of the blue. Whenever I feel one coming on, I relax my shoulders and the muscles in my face and take a few deep breaths. I notice what emotions I'm feeling, what thoughts I'm thinking, and what's going on in the rest of my body. Sometimes I just spent a lot of time staring at my phone and started thinking about how I'm going to give myself one. Other times I'm feeling stress, anger, frustration, or worry and it's causing tension of some kind in my body. I can usually feel my leg, hip, and shoulder muscles tensed up like they're forming a barrier and keeping the emotion locked in, which creates pressure in my head. So I focus on feeling the emotion and releasing it. And since that time, I've been able to successfully stave off a headache every time. It's completely changed the quality of my life.

The only person who can really cure you is you. You create your circumstances. Since you chose them, you can change your mind and un-choose them too. Decide that healing is more appealing than illness. Rather than focus on your illness, focus on visualizing and feeling a life of health and vitality. Be that person who has a great attitude no matter what life throws their way.

What you believe will cure you is what will cure you, but you have to make up your mind that you want to heal. You have to have the intention of healing. If you believe Western medicine doctors will help you, then you're much more likely to heal after that pill. If you believe a vegan diet can cure you, then it can. If you believe Chinese medicine will cure you, then it will. But the truth is that you don't need anyone other than yourself. Your body knows how to heal itself. That's why the placebo effect is so powerful. Your body is responding to your thoughts and your beliefs.

When we think about the placebo effect we tend to think about pills. And in fact, Irving Kirsch, Associate Director of the Program in Placebo Studies and a lecturer in medicine at the Harvard Medical School, found that 80 percent of the positive effects that anti-depressants have on patients could be attributed to the placebo effect.[6] But the placebo effect's powers go way beyond pills.

Baylor School of Medicine published a study in 2002 in the New English Journal of Medicine about an experiment that tested out the placebo effect's impact on surgery. Dr. Bruce Moseley, the orthopedic knee surgeon who authored the study, conducted a test in which he divided patients into three groups. None of the patients knew which type of surgery they would be receiving and weren't told for two years after receiving it. During surgery on the first group, he merely cleaned debris out of the patients' knees. For the second group, he shaved off some of their bone. With the third group he *pretended* to do surgery. He prepped the knee, asked his assistants to hand him instruments, made the same incisions as he had for the prior groups, even splashed saline solution onto the area for effect, and then stitched the patients back up. All three groups were sent home with the same recovery instructions, including physical therapy. The results were impressive. Patients in the placebo group healed just as well as

---

6   Irving Kirsch PhD, *The Emperor's New Drugs: Exploding the Antidepressant Myth* (Basic Books, Reprint edition, March 8, 2011)

those in the other two groups, no longer used canes, reported less knee pain, and went on to live active lives.[7]

Harvard Professor of Psychology Ellen Langer conducted a radical experiment in 1979 where she took eight men in their seventies and put them into a house decorated to look like it was 1959. The Ed Sullivan show played on the TV, newspapers and magazines from the era littered the space, popular fifties tunes filled the air, and all of the décor was from the time period. Stepping through the door was like going into a time warp. The men stayed there for five days and were instructed to act as though it really was 1959. They wore clothing from the time period, they talked about historical events as if they were current news, and photos of their younger selves sat on their nightstands. There were no mirrors in the house and no mention of or accommodation for the men's physical state; no one helped them with their luggage or gave them a hand up the stairs. An array of physical tests were done before and after and a control group stayed in a similar house but weren't instructed to act as though it were 1959. After only five days they found the men's vision improved, they had better intelligence scores, they stood up taller, and they looked younger. They even played an impromptu game of touch football on the lawn. They outperformed the control group on every test. Langer commented, "They put their minds in an earlier time and their bodies went along for the ride." Thirty years later the BBC recreated the experiment with a group of elderly celebrities in a mini-series called *The Young Ones* that they aired on TV and got

---

7   J. Bruce Moseley, Kimberly O'Malley, Nancy J. Petersen, et al, "A Controlled Trial of Arthroscopic Surgery for Osteoarthritis of the Knee" *N Engl J Med*, 347 (Jul 11, 2002): 81-88

the same results. One man arrived in a wheelchair and left using only a cane and another who couldn't even get dressed without assistance threw a dinner party on the final night. Everyone left standing taller, feeling more energetic, and looking physically younger.

Gregg Braden writes in *The Isaiah Effect* about an amazing video he was shown while in China. The video took place at the Huaxia Zhineng Qigong Clinic & Training Center and shows three healers in a room with a woman who has bladder cancer. She is lying next to an ultrasound machine, and on the machine you can clearly see the tumor. The three men around her begin to meditate and chant a single word that roughly translates in English to "already gone." Braden describes the awesome moment that he watches the tumor start to quiver and then fade from view while the rest of the image on the screen stays in focus. After that, Western-style doctors could no longer detect cancer in the patient. The intentions of the healers and the belief of the patient made it happen.

While most people have heard of the placebo effect, few have heard of its counterpart, the nocebo effect. The nocebo effect tells us that a negative thought, including a belief that we are vulnerable to a condition or have been exposed to a toxic substance, can actually manifest pain and illness. The nocebo effect is just as powerful in controlling our health as the placebo effect is. Cell biologist Bruce Lipton points out that when we think about the fact that one third of all medical healings are attributed to the placebo effect and that psychologists say 70 percent of our thoughts are negative and repetitive, this has serious implications. How much of our pain and illness are we causing with our negative thoughts?

Your body has an incredible capacity to heal itself once everything falls into alignment. Your body's natural state is one of health, and this is the state it wants to be at. Illness only shows up to tell you something is off. Your body is simply showing you what your mind and emotions are feeling because you either aren't aware or you haven't been paying attention. Once you heal emotionally, your body will follow suit quickly and with ease, requiring practically no effort on your part.

You don't need to fight anything (whether it's illness or any other life circumstance). When you fight these things, you give more energy to them and the cycle continues. Instead, heal your inner world and focus on what you do want and pour all of your attention and energy into that.

Pay attention to how you categorize or explain an illness as well. Sometimes we call something genetic without there being any real meaning behind that word. Beliefs and thought patterns can travel through generational lines. Maybe your great- great-great-grandmother had negative thoughts about something or had a life lesson to learn and it manifested as a certain illness. Then when her daughter was around that age and had the slightest sign of an illness, her mind jumped to "this is how old mom was when she had this thing. It must be that." And then she manifests it. And with every generation the belief grows stronger and stronger because they have all this "proof" of the generations before. You can be the person in your family to break that cycle.

And sometimes illness is a choice you've made before you're reincarnated, for your own benefit. Remember, we choose big life events that we will go through that will help us learn lessons and grow. Through her work, Dolores Cannon uncovered that souls line up to be incarnated into handicap bodies because the amount of growth and lessons they receive from that single life is exponentially greater that way. They accelerate through the school of Earth much faster because of their experience.

And sometimes the illness or pain is the lesson that someone must go through to fulfill their soul contract and learn the lesson they were meant to learn in this lifetime. Sometimes the lesson is also for the loved ones of the person, and they agreed to go through it before they incarnated as well. This is why sometimes babies get cancer, not everyone has miraculous spontaneous healings, and some people spend years as caretakers for their sick relatives. It sounds cruel or unfair from our point of view on 3D Earth when we cannot see the whole picture. But no doubt, from an expanded frame of reference on the other side of the veil, it makes complete sense. Remember that nothing here on our planet can hurt one's true self, we are here to have experiences, and there are multiple versions of you across multiple time lines. Chances are there is a version of you who passed away at every age possible from infancy to old age, ones who are sick, ones who have healed, and so on. You are here to experience it all. But it doesn't mean you should give in to your circumstances because you can always change your mind, make a different choice, and change the trajectory of your life. Big life circumstances are predetermined, but free will still exists.

Change your mind about the way you view pain and illness and opportunities to heal will open up before you.

Pathways to Healing

Now let's talk about ways to heal and clear out repressed emotions, negativity, and trauma the body stores that are affecting the quality of your life. First, you need to decide you want to change. Only you can truly decide that, and you won't truly change until you are 100 percent committed to doing so. If some outside influence is what's telling you to change, then it likely won't happen. You might start and make some progress, but ultimately you'll wind up back where you started. You need to make the conscious choice to stop doing things that hurt you, to let go of things that no longer serve you, and to start focusing on things that heal you.

One powerful, little exercise I like to do to release negative thoughts anytime they show up is to imagine them in my mind's eye like they're a piece of paper, and then I imagine crumpling them up and throwing them away, off into the abyss. Once they get a certain distance, I imagine them exploding into dust and then the particles dissolving into the air without a trace. It's a way to stop negative thoughts in their tracks and then release them without even giving them the time of day.

The key to releasing repressed emotions is to truly feel them. Once you do, they very quickly dissipate and then are gone forever. You don't have to carry them around with you anymore. Typically, the emotions are layered, so the one on the surface that you're feeling isn't really the true root emotion that became repressed. As you start to let go of the top layer of emotion, it quickly morphs into another one, and eventually what is below at the deepest point is uncovered. For example, extreme rage is often covering up sadness, and when you allow yourself to feel your rage, it can morph into deep heartache.

Being told to just "go feel your repressed emotions" can be confusing. Where do you even start? And how do you do that? Especially when you're not even sure what you're repressing.

Physical modalities are a great way to move energy throughout your body, to shake loose things that have been stuck for a long time and then to let them go. If you get to a point where you can physically exhaust your body and mind, then the emotions will flow out.

Here are some of the most powerful ways I've found to release all that junk that we carry around:

1. Osho's Dynamic Meditation

If you're like many people, you might have a hard time sitting still and quieting your mind in meditation. I have a brother-in-law who sits in meditation for five hours every day, loves going to Vipassana retreats (ten-day silent retreats where you sit in meditation for the majority of the day, don't speak a word to anyone the whole time, and don't even make eye contact with other people), and spends many months each year meditating with monks in the Himalayas. I think it's amazing that he does these things, but that will never be me. And I don't think that it will ever be most of us, which is totally okay. We live in a modern, fast-paced, digital world that is rapidly speeding up. Bite-sized self-care rituals and opportunities to go within where movement is involved fit much better into most of our lives.

When meditation first became a thing among the yogis, the people were on their feet working all day in the fields. So when they got home, it was easy to sit and be still in meditation. We've flipped that relationship with movement and stillness in modern society. Many of us spend much of the day sitting at our computers for work, and by the end of the day, we can't sit any longer. We are antsy and crave movement and need to get all of our restless pent-up energy out. Osho created his dynamic meditation for precisely this reason.

When I was running a yoga teacher training, I had the pleasure of working with a couple from Washington named Subhan and Shanti who lived with and studied directly under Osho. While I know Osho's ranch is a controversial topic, I urge you to separate the teachings from the actions of some of the followers. Even when you disagree with the actions of the mystics and teachers themselves, their teachings have the potential to stand alone as gifts to the world. The example I often use is with the hot yoga practice made popular in the Western world by Bikram Choudhury. You can feel whatever you want about Bikram himself and still love the yoga he introduced to the world.

Osho's Dynamic Meditation is a one-hour experience broken into five parts. It's set to very specific music that cues the change in parts, and you are blindfolded the entire time. It is one of the most powerful exercises I've ever done. The most important part, to me, is the second part which is the "catharsis." It only lasts ten minutes, but it's amazing how much you release.

The first part, a breathing exercise, primes your body for this catharsis. It works deep to dig loose anything that is stuck. I always imagine someone is taking a spoon and scraping away black tar (all of the negative junk and emotions I've accumulated) from inside my chest cavity. The more you commit to the breathing exercise, the more you'll be able to release in the catharsis stage. By the time the music changes to cue it's time for catharsis, the tension is so built up that it just explodes out of you. You can't even help it. It's hard to describe, but it's incredible and so, so powerful. Dynamic Meditation is typically practiced in a group setting and when you get to the catharsis, it's like wild banshees have been let loose. Everyone starts screaming, swearing, crying, wailing, laughing, giggling, yawning, stretching, stomping, and anything else they have the urge to do. It's about a release of *any* kind, and as long as you don't hurt yourself or anyone else, then anything goes. The next part snaps you out of the catharsis so you can completely let go of that state.

If you're going to try dynamic meditation, I highly encourage you to do it in a group setting led by someone who is experienced. It's not really the type of exercise you do on your own, at least not the first couple of times. If you're interested in trying out dynamic meditation with Subhan and Shanti, they run The World of Meditation Center in Washington state and as of this writing, have some offerings online as well if you're unable to travel there. They are two truly special human beings. I don't know if you've ever had the experience of looking into someone's eyes and feeling such a depth of love and wisdom and such a kind soul emanating from them, but that is my experience with Subhan and Shanti. I feel blessed and grateful to call them two of my teachers.

2. Yoga

Yoga can have a similar effect. As a yoga teacher, I've personally seen how healing the practice can be. I've seen people overcome injuries, accidents, emotional trauma, poor body image, illness, and so much more through their yoga practice. I can't tell you how many times my students have cried through my yoga classes because they were releasing some deep wound or working through a current stressor in their life. And I can't tell you how many times I have sobbed my way through one as well.

Yoga can allow trauma survivors to understand how their body deals with their emotions and help them find a way to feel their emotions so they don't keep repressing them. In *The Body Keeps the Score*, the author talks about a rape survivor suffering from PTSD who decided to try yoga. At first just simply being touched on the back made her jump and feel triggered. But as she kept practicing, she realized that her body was clueing her in to her emotional state. As she practiced, feelings and sensations such as sadness, pain, and vulnerability bubbled up to the surface but instead of pushing those feelings away, she began to feel them so that she could ultimately let them go.

Having a regular yoga practice is a good way to chip away at these repressed emotions. When we practice yoga, we're moving energy, and little by little these pockets get released as we keep working deeper and deeper into ourselves. What I like about dynamic meditation is that it blasts it out of you all at once. Of course, that's not to say that you do it once and you're "healed" or "cured." There's always more to go and deeper layers to be felt and released. But it does get you there faster. Yoga is the more gentle approach. I recommend a healthy mix of both practices.

If you find yourself having a knee-jerk reaction that you don't enjoy yoga, I encourage you to try out several types of yoga until you find one that speaks to you. There are tons of types out there, from slow Hatha where you hold poses a long time, to rigid, alignment-based Ashtanga where you must master each pose before you're able to move on to the next, to Traditional Hot Yoga which is practiced in 105-degree heat and 40 percent humidity, to Yin where you're on the floor the entire time and don't engage your muscles at all so that you can instead work into your fascia, to quick-paced Power Vinyasa Flows which link breath to movement. And if your excuse is that you aren't flexible, then let me quickly point out the fact that flexibility is not the point of yoga and you absolutely do not have to be flexible to start a yoga practice. When I first started practicing, I could barely touch my knees, let alone my toes. Yoga is another path inward, a moving meditation, a way to release repressed emotions and connect your mind, body, and spirit. Flexibility and muscle tone are just happy side effects that come along with a regular yoga practice. I like to tell my students that it's a "work-in" as well as a workout. Traditionally, yogis practiced the poses to exhaust their body and mind in order to find deeper silence and peace in their meditation practice.

I know that starting a yoga practice can be very intimidating for a lot of people. I used to be uncomfortable in yoga studios when I first started out. I felt like every other person in the class had a perfect yoga body and a perfect yoga outfit and a practice that made them look like they belonged on the cover of *Yoga Journal* magazine. I hated when teachers would single me out in classes and correct my poses because it made me feel like I was bad at yoga.

It wasn't until I walked into the studio I would eventually go on to manage that I felt safe in a yoga space, like I was coming home. The classes were donation-based so they appealed to a wide variety of people. There was every walk of life in the classes, from elderly to teenagers, homeless people to wealthy tech entrepreneurs, every race, every socio-economic status, every gender, every sexual orientation, every body type. There were hippies and punk rockers and everything in between. People showed up in whatever kind of clothing they felt comfortable moving in. There were no judgments of any kind. Everyone was just there to get their yoga in. There were no mirrors in the room. During class, the teachers encouraged us to close our eyes, to not worry too much about what poses looked like—it was more about how we felt inside of them. The best part to me was that I could get lost in the crowd. I could be having a bad day and go into the middle of the room, anonymous in a room full of strangers, and cry and no one would even bat an eye. I quickly realized that there was something profound changing within me as I continued to show up for class. It became my safe place, my church. It became a spiritual practice for me, a moving meditation, a release. I felt drawn to my mat almost daily. And at the end of class I would lie in savasana and my body and mind would be exhausted and emptied out and, just for a bit, my muscles were completely relaxed and there were no thoughts, like my mind was a blank slate and I could just float and drift in pure peace and relaxation and inner stillness.

If that sounds appealing to you, I have recreated this experience at Unite By Yoga, the studio I now own.

3. TRE

TRE (Tension, Stress, Trauma Release) is another powerful modality that is gaining traction. It is a series of exercises you perform that trigger a shaking response in your body. You know how you tremble when you get scared or anxious? Well, it turns out that response is a healthy one your body does to release excess tension built up in your muscles. When we have stress and negative emotions like fear, we tend to subconsciously tuck our tailbone under, much like a scared dog. When you perform the exact exercises with a TRE trainer, they stimulate this same shaking response and help reverse that tucking and release any tension built up as a result of it. It tends to focus more on the tension built up in the physical body rather than the emotional body though, so I still like to pair it with a yoga and dynamic meditation practice.

4. Vocalizations

If I don't have time for a full dynamic meditation or yoga practice, one of my absolute favorite things to do is make any kind of vocalizations, such as primal screaming, om-ing, or just letting my body make any weird, animalistic noise it wants to. When I do this, I can literally feel the vibrations in my chest shaking loose any tension, and I can feel it escaping out of my body. Shane and I will often lay in bed and make weird noises at the end of a stressful day. It helps so much. Drop your ego and don't worry about sounding weird. We're animals—let the sounds your body naturally makes help heal you.

5. Hypnosis

Beyond these physical activities, hypnosis is a tool I have relied deeply on in my own healing journey with profound results. This includes the Quantum Healing Hypnosis Technique (QHHT) developed by Dolores Cannon when performed by a qualified practitioner and Jose Silva's self-hypnosis technique that he teaches in his book *You the Healer*.

Jose Silva's technique is done by lying down, taking yourself through a body relaxation technique, looking up at your third eye with your eyes closed, smoothing out your breath, and counting yourself backward into an alpha-brain state.

At some point, you'll notice a shift. What happens will be personal to you. For me, what I see behind my closed eyelids changes. The background color shifts and I start to see slow swirls of color moving in a hypnotic pattern. Sometimes I see circles that slowly ebb and flow, expand and contract, to the rhythm of my breath. My jaw muscles get slack and heavy. My head gets heavy. My limbs get heavy. And then I forget that I have limbs. I'm no longer aware of my body at all. I am just pure, floating consciousness and it is peaceful and calm and warm and safe. What you notice is yours and yours alone. You'll know the shift when it happens. You are now in an alpha- brain wave state. The state of daydreaming and transitioning into sleep. But you're not asleep yet. This is the state that hypnotists put you in. You can stay lingering in this state for as long as you'd like. You can use this as a platform to get into deep meditation and then just drift off into space from this soothing place. You can use it to heal physical or emotional ailments. You can use it to visualize scenes from your

Manifest Memoir to help stamp them into your subconscious. You can also use it as a tool to put yourself to sleep.

Whatever method(s) you find work for you, keep using them. However old you are is how many years of repressed emotions have likely been building up inside of you, so it takes time to release them all. You'll go deeper and deeper into your core, like peeling away the layers of an onion. I often find during dynamic meditation that old memories I didn't even know I had stored in my mind will be brought to the forefront and I'll relive them so clearly, as though I'm there again. And not just negative ones, happy ones too. It's all there, stored in the library of your mind, for you to explore. And as new feelings and emotions come up, really allow yourself the time and space to feel them so you can then let them go. We're feeling beings and our emotions are meant to be felt fully and then released. We're not designed to obsessively cling to negative emotions like anger, guilt, and sadness and to keep reliving the past. All that does is bring us pain in the present moment and eventually possibly disease.

Being spiritual doesn't mean that you have to always think positive thoughts and ignore the negative ones that show up. We're meant to participate in and feel the entire gamut of this human experience. So allow yourself to unapologetically be a human being. Feel it all fully. And then let it all go so you can move forward to the next experience.

CHAPTER 8

MOVING FORWARD INTO
THE LIFE YOU DESIRE

I want to just take a moment to pause and acknowledge how far we've come together. You've learned to broaden your view of what reality is and how it is malleable and moldable and how you can use the powers you were born with to create the results you want to see. We've talked about adding positive habits to your daily life such as mantras and journaling, and how to let go of emotions and thoughts that only weigh you down and potentially even cause you harm. We've covered forgiving others and ourselves and how you can rewire your brain when it comes to how you think about illness and pain. And you've mapped out the blueprint for what your future will look like with your Manifest Memoir. You've changed your mind when it comes to your health, the world, the people you encounter, reality, and so much more. You've come quite a long way!

Bringing It All Together

If you've gotten this far, you might be asking, "What now?"

This chapter is all about taking action steps to move forward. So many Law of Attraction books out there talk about manifesting as if the universe were a genie in a bottle, and you can ask it for what you want and then sit back and kick your feet up to wait while it comes to you. Manifesting, journaling, and getting clear on your vision is an important piece of the puzzle, but it's not the *whole* piece. Oftentimes I've seen these other books neglect that it's important to take steps to make your dreams a reality. You need to call them into action.

They say it takes twenty-one days to form a new habit and, if you follow my recommendations for this amount of time, you'll be completely flushing all of the toxins out of your life and injecting it with all of the good, new energy. You'll be letting go of habits that no longer serve you and creating positive ones to fill their place all at once. It's like a cleansing of your life. This program isn't meant to be stopped after twenty-one days, but rather I'd like you to think of it as a twenty-one-day intensive reset so that the habits continue effortlessly afterward without you having to put much thought into it while it all becomes second nature for you.

So now it's time to move forward to utilize all of this knowledge and this new mindset that you've gained.

- Every night before bed for the next twenty-one days, read your Manifest Memoir. Every time something additional comes up that you really want to manifest, journal about it using the three-part journaling technique you learned in chapter 4.

- Every morning for the next twenty-one days, write down something you're grateful for. These gratitude entries are best to do when you first wake up in the morning because starting your day in the frequency of gratitude is energizing and aligning.

- Continue to write down any thoughts that show you what you want, where you feel unfulfilled, and what you're fearful of. And then use the FEAR journaling exercise we learned in the last chapter once a week.

- Work on releasing repressed emotions with whatever means resonated most with you. And allow yourself to feel all of the emotions that show up in your life.

- If more feelings come up around a perceived wrongdoing that was either done to you or you did, practice forgiving yourself and others. Maybe even reread the chapter about forgiveness. Sometimes it takes a few times for all of the information to get absorbed.

Put these exercises into practice and watch how your world transforms. But this next part is just as important.

Take Action

Without taking action, you become stuck and uninspired. Action requires movement, which moves energy, which inspires the universe to make movement back for you. Visualize your dreams and journal on them and get really clear on your vision to help call them into your life, but then also act on them. And oftentimes it doesn't even have to be huge movements on your part. Sometimes just taking a small step is enough to put a chain of events into motion.

I want to clarify quickly that taking action doesn't mean you have to work hard. I don't believe that at all, and in fact, it irks me when people say you only achieve your dreams with hard work. Taking action is about taking a step in the direction of your dream life. There is something magical that takes place when you outline where you want your life to go and then start to move energy by taking a step toward that place. It's like adding on the finishing touches, the last ingredient in a spell, the fairy dust on top. It awakens something within the universe. It kickstarts it. You start to create the tiniest bit of movement, and the universe responds with building momentum and takes it over from there, whooshing you forward further and faster than you could have imagined.

So pull out your Manifest Memoir and get out a blank piece of paper. Start to read your Manifest Memoir again. For each thing you are calling into your life, write one action item you can do right now to move you in the direction of that dream on the blank sheet of paper. Keep in mind that it's not something you can do once something else happens, but something you can do right now with the resources available to you at this exact moment in time. When you're finished, you should have at least one action item for every single thing in your Manifest Memoir.

If you're feeling overwhelmed by this, relax and remember that it doesn't have to be a massive undertaking at first. Don't underestimate the power of a small step. From one small step, new ideas may flow to you. You might meet new people you wouldn't have otherwise met who can help you on your path. That one step might put you in the right position to achieve your dream, a whole world might become unlocked and available to you. You just never know.

So if manifesting a partner is on your list, then maybe you sign up for a dating app or go to a social event. If getting a dog is on your list, then maybe you visit a shelter or start researching breeds. If writing a book is on your list, then maybe you start to work on an outline. If losing weight is on your list, maybe you go buy some healthy groceries and toss out the junk food in your cabinets. If moving to a new town is on your list, then maybe you start researching jobs or housing in a new place.

The point is that there is always *something* you can do to lead you one step closer to the life you truly desire. You're never so stuck in one place that there's no way out and nothing you can do. Things don't have to be perfect, and the timing doesn't have to be right for you to start. There is always *something* you can do from the place you're at with the resources you have available. If you can't think of a single step, you're not looking at it from a broad enough perspective. Try working with a life coach to get a different point of view and help kickstart the creative flow of ideas. There are usually many more options than you can initially see.

Next, take that step! That's the important part. Manifest it and then start to put energy toward it by taking a step, and the universe will move mountains to make it happen in unexpected ways. Remember to become obsessed with the thing that you want. Research it like crazy, immerse yourself in it wholeheartedly. Don't get discouraged, and don't get bored. Spend your free time working toward it, reading about it, doing it, whatever *it* is. And put your whole self into it. Don't just give it a half-ass, lazy piece of your energy. This is your *dream life* that we're talking about—give it the energy it deserves!

After you've done the first step over the course of the first week, take another step in the second week. And it's okay to have multiple plates spinning if you have multiple things you're trying to attract. However, if that ever feels overwhelming, it's also okay to pull back and focus on just one area of your Manifest Memoir at a time. Whatever works best for you so that you don't get discouraged or stressed out. Remember, this is supposed to be fun! Make life into a game.

Then create a calendar for yourself moving forward of when you are going to carve out time to take steps toward your dream life. If you're anything like me, you live by your calendar because you're so busy, so schedule it in advance to make sure you are setting aside time for it, even if it's just fifteen minutes each day. Every day, do something to move toward your goals and better your life, even if it's just doing something small that makes you smile or feel happy on the tough days.

Put it into your calendar to hold yourself accountable and then keep the appointment with yourself. That's the important part! Don't schedule other meetings during that time. Don't use that time to take a break or browse social media. Show up for yourself and show up big. It's the best form of self-love there is. Which brings us to our next topic...

Self-Care

Another important thing to work into your schedule is self-care. These days we can get so swept up in our jobs, social lives, families, kids, and partners that we forget to really slow down and do things that make us feel good and are good for us. Prioritize yourself! When you are properly taking care of yourself, you're healthier and have more vitality, and this makes your manifesting all the more powerful. Plus, as the old saying goes, you can't pour from an empty cup. Here are five categories for self-care. Try to hit something from each list each day. If none of the things I list out appeal to you, then do something else you love for each category. If you've never heard of some of these things, then try them! Remember, getting out of your comfort zone is *good* for you and is where growth happens!

1. Delight Your Senses Every Day

Relax and release tension daily.

- take a warm bath
- use essential oils
- listen to a guided meditation
- go to a sound healing meditation
- practice self-hypnosis on yourself
- get a reiki treatment
- get a massage
- read an uplifting book
- watch an uplifting documentary

- listen to relaxing music

- get an acupuncture treatment

- practice pranayama (breath work)

- laugh with your best friend

- go to a bhakti yoga session where you get to chant

- get a network spinal analysis session

- listen to binaural beats

- om a few times

All of these things reduce stress, calm your nervous system, bring you into a parasympathetic state (rest, digest, and create), and boost your immune system as a result.

When you don't take the time to find relaxation every day, tension becomes built up and repressed. And when your body is under stress and in a sympathetic state (fight, flight, or freeze), you're unable to do crucial things like digest, detox, and heal.

Try to get out in the sun for twenty minutes every day, especially in the morning, to soak up the beneficial red light. Invest in blue blocking glasses for the evening time as you start to wind down. This will help your circadian rhythm, melatonin production, and so much more.

Red light (infrared light) from the sun first thing in the morning stimulates collagen, increases bone healing, and heals wounds. It is proven to be anti-aging and reduces wrinkles and scars. Infrared light around sunrise preconditions our skin to protect us from the UVA and UVB that comes out a bit later, so you're less likely to burn later in the day, which is important because you need to soak up some vitamin D through the daytime sun. Later morning sun is critical in making nitric oxide, the same thing we release when we exercise. It also increases energy and memory and is anti-aging. Finally, it triggers the production of serotonin and dopamine and releases endorphins, making us feel good.

Artificial blue light, such as that found in our electronics screens, can cause myopia (short-sightedness), macular degeneration (blindness), obesity, diabetes, brain degeneration, hormonal issues, and so much more. It also messes up your sleep patterns by disrupting your natural melatonin production if you watch TV or look at your phone or computer at night, which is why I recommend wearing blue blocking glasses in the evening.

Anything you can do to stimulate your vagus nerve is always good. Your vagus nerve plays a major part in stress relief. It has around 100,000 parasympathetic nerve fibers that connect with your brain, then it wanders past your voice box and runs down your body, touching every major organ on its way down. It's the longest and most complex cranial nerve in your body and the primary component of your parasympathetic nervous system. Interestingly, it also activates your gut microbiome, which can modulate inflammation and affect your brain and behavior. Things like singing, humming, taking vibrational breaths, and primal screaming can all stimulate your vagus nerve and release tension from your body. It's pretty wild! This is why when I teach my yoga class, I teach vibrational breaths too:

H-A-Haaas, H-M-Hmmmms, flutters of your lips, and so on. They recalibrate your nervous system, release heat and tension from your body, and stimulate your vagus nerve.

2. Eat Food That's Good for You

I struggled about whether or not to include this section because while it's a topic I'm passionate about and believe many people will find helpful, I also don't want to promote fear in any way. So I decided the best way to do it is to present my experience and research on the subject matter and then turn it all on its head and talk about food from a completely different perspective. So first let's look at the science:

First things first, treat your body well! It's your one and only vehicle for moving through this lifetime, and just like you wouldn't neglect your car when it needs new brakes or an oil change, it's important to take care of it. The better your diet, the better you will feel and the more energy you will have to create your dream life and do all the things you love to do. Try cutting out sugar and processed foods as a place to start. If you want to really dive in and commit, release gluten from your diet as well, at least for the twenty-one days.

Gluten can lead to thyroid issues, including Hashimoto's, where your body attacks your thyroid gland. This is because, on a molecular level, gluten looks very similar to the thyroid hormone. Your body tries to attack all of the gluten and ends up attacking your thyroid in the process, seeing it as a foreign invader also. Gluten also causes inflammation and has wheat germ agglutinin, which makes nutrients unusable by your body. According to Dr. Will Cole, this can cause an immune response, leading to chronic systemic inflammation. Gluten can cause leaky gut, where your gut lining becomes permeable, and food particles, toxins, and bacteria get through the holes and into your bloodstream. This causes inflammation which can lead to a host of autoimmune disorders.

Dairy can do similar things to some people because it can cross-react with gluten, meaning that your body will respond to dairy the same way it does to gluten. This is because the protein found in dairy is so similar to the protein found in gluten that your body can't tell the difference between the two. If you're gluten intolerant, you might suffer from:

a wide range of autoimmune conditions

skin conditions like eczema and acne

fatigue

joint pain

arthritis

bloating

gas

heartburn

constipation

diarrhea

anxiety

irritability

moodiness

chronic headaches

migraines

brain fog (which is inflammation in your brain)

trouble focusing

decreased memory function

neurological conditions

depression

anxiety

There have even been studies done that link gluten and sugar to autism, ADD, and ADHD.

I have suffered from bad eczema my entire life. It moved around my body every few years, but I would get it across my elbows, on my hands, and my legs mostly. I would be broken out in itchy red bumps and blotches almost constantly, and the harsh Chicago winters where I grew up only amplified the irritations. My hands were always bright red, and I would wake myself up scratching in my sleep. My skin would crack and form cuts, and the skin around the bumps would become inflamed. It was miserable. Doctors would prescribe me tubes of steroid cream, and for well over a decade, I would slather steroid cream onto my body daily. The steroids were like a Band-Aid. They kept the itchiness at bay but never got rid of the eczema completely. The moment I stopped using it, it would flare up again.

When I was in my mid-twenties, the book *Wheat Belly* by Dr. William Davis came out and became a sensation. That was the first time I learned about the perils of gluten. The book focused mostly on how eliminating gluten will cause you to lose weight (think wheat belly instead of beer belly), but there were a few lines in there that I zoomed in on about how gluten can affect your skin and cause things like eczema. I decided to cut gluten out. It was awful at first. I went through terrible withdrawals and cravings. I was super moody, super lethargic, and had super bad brain fog. All I wanted were bagels and cookies and cake and noodles and bread. But I stuck with it. It took six weeks for the gluten to get out of my system, but as soon as it did, my skin cleared up. My eczema was finally gone. And it's never come back. I threw out all of my steroid creams and did a happy dance. I've tested it out plenty of times too. The moment I eat gluten again, it's like a light switch and the eczema comes back. I couldn't help but think at the time that if gluten was doing that to my skin, the outermost organ of my body, what was it doing to my insides? I've been gluten-free for ten years now, and I don't even miss it. And gluten-free snacks and recipes have gotten so good I don't even notice the difference anymore.

You don't have to have such obvious outward signs to have a gluten sensitivity. The damage could be purely internal. It's worth getting a food sensitivity test (different than an allergy test) from a functional medicine doctor. Or better yet, go gluten-free for six weeks and see how you feel.

"What about other grains?" you might ask. Grains have a reputation for being a superfood (think of the old school food pyramid with grains on the bottom row), but they can also destroy your health. Plants like grains don't want to be eaten, so they've developed a defense system called lectins to protect themselves. Lectins can cause inflammation, leaky gut, weight gain, and excessive hunger in human beings.

Some types of lectins can prevent your body from absorbing nutrients, leading to malnutrition. Other sources of lectins are considered seriously toxic. Legumes such as beans, lentils, peas, peanuts, and soybeans also contain a high amount of lectins. Dr. Will Cole tells us that grains not only contain lectins but also enzyme inhibitors (which make it difficult for your body to break down food), phytic acid (antinutrients that bind to minerals and make them unusable), amylose (sugar found in grains that will spike your blood sugar), and omega-6 fatty acids (which are highly inflammatory when out of balance with omega-3s). To me, it's not worth it.

I personally follow a paleo diet and work closely with my good friend who is a functional medicine doctor to see where my lab work is at on a regular basis. I also take a lot of supplements to keep my labs at optimal levels. I've found the best thing to do is eat fresh, clean, whole food whenever possible, like plenty of organic vegetables, some organic fruit, healthy fats like olive oil and avocado, lots of filtered water, and, if you eat meat, then grass fed and finished meats and wild-caught, low mercury seafood. A lot of the negative things you hear about what meat can do to your body is talking about meat where the animal is grain fed. Grain fed meat is awful for you while grass fed meat is not. If you must occasionally eat a small amount of grain, then I recommend making it a gluten-free grain and make sure it is a whole grain and not refined grain. Whole grains contain the entire grain seed in their original proportions, so your body has to work to break them down, meaning they digest more slowly and don't cause as big of a spike in your blood sugar. Taking a digestive enzyme with them can help even more. If you are craving bread, try making your own sourdough and see if you can tolerate that. Sourdough bread contains lower amounts of gluten, lower levels of antinutrients, and more prebiotics. Plus, it will rise naturally as opposed to containing the quick yeast most bread manufacturers use nowadays, which many people can't tolerate.

If you need to have one goal, then I suggest it be to balance out and stabilize your blood sugar. Eating foods high in sugar causes your body to respond with a rapid rise and then dramatic fall in blood sugar levels. This rollercoaster, and having high blood sugar in general, can lead to inflammation, hormone disruption, and insulin resistance. These three conditions can cause a host of problems, such as trouble sleeping, trouble concentrating, increased fat storage, mental health and mood disorders, more food cravings, brain fog, susceptibility to illness, thyroid issues, and much more. Chronic high blood glucose can lead to even more serious instances such as heart disease and stroke, type 2 diabetes, high blood pressure, obesity, kidney disease, vision problems, and nerve problems. Plus, sugar feeds things like cancer and bad bacteria and yeast in your gut.

Every system in your body can be negatively impacted by sugar but especially your gut microbiome, your endocrine system, and your nervous system. It can even weaken your immune system. Simply eating 75 grams of sugar can lower your immune response for five hours.

The goal should be to maintain homeostasis where you're on a smooth, even keel throughout the day with blood sugar gently rising and slowly lowering as you eat. You can invest in a glucose meter and check each morning on an empty stomach and then periodically throughout the day to see which foods spike your blood sugar. Aim for a fasting (first thing in the morning) blood sugar in the 70s-90s.

If you love baking and are feeling disheartened by all of this, try using almond flour or coconut flour and stevia as a sweetener since it won't spike your blood sugar. Even a little bit of honey is better than sugar. You also don't have to deprive yourself all the time. Moderation is key. Yes, I indulge in sweets every so often.

All of this will make you feel like you have superpowers. You'll be buzzing with energy, you'll feel light, and you'll feel satiated without feeling bloated or overstuffed. At the same time, you'll feel much more calm and clear-headed. Food is medicine. Take care of your body, feed it good fuel, so that you feel good. When your body feels good, you have more power to manifest and focus on things that bring you joy.

You might get cravings at first if this type of diet is new to you, as gluten and sugar can both act like drugs in your body and put you into a state of withdrawal for the first several weeks. But if you stick with it, you'll start to notice that your cravings go away, your anxiety goes down, and so does your inflammation while your energy and vitality will go up. Your body will be fed the right foods so that it can do what it's made to do and heal itself.

I highly recommend seeing a functional medicine doctor. Functional medicine is different than traditional Western medicine because it treats the root causes, not just the symptoms. It's worth it even to just get your labs checked routinely because they'll test for a lot more than your regular Western medicine doctor will and then come up with a personal diet and supplement plan for you. My good friend, Dr. Taylor Krick, is a functional medicine doctor who sees patients virtually from all over the country. He doesn't believe in hiking up the cost for lab work, so he'll charge you what he pays himself. His podcast, *The Autoimmune Doc Podcast*, and YouTube channel are both invaluable resources and you can find the links for both in the "Learn More" section in the back of the book.

So now that I've said all of that, I'm going to seemingly contradict myself because the number one most important thing is this: Eat in ways that make you feel good but out of self-love rather than out of fear. Remember the way you feel about yourself and the world is what's going to reflect in your body. So if you're choosing to not eat certain foods because you're afraid they're going to cause disease, you're doing it out of fear and that fear will be much more harmful to you than that food ever could be.

If you're eating all organic vegetarian foods as a punishment to yourself or as a way to avoid punishment from others, then that same energy you're reflecting will come back to you and you're doing more harm than good. If you choose to have a hot fudge sundae because it fills you with joy and is a way of showering yourself with love, then that is a great choice. But if you're eating that sundae and then feel bad about yourself or guilty later, then that defeats the purpose.

I personally feel my best when I eat mostly vegetables and fruits, with healthy fats, a tiny bit of meat, and little to no grain and legumes. It's all about finding what works best for your body while being mindful of your reasons for choices and the emotions they stem from. I also think a vegetarian or vegan diet is a wonderful choice, so long as you're not supplementing with a bunch of refined grains and legumes that are high in lectins. And, of course, it's always important to work with your own licensed health care practitioner to make the right choices for your body and circumstances.

3. Cleanse Your Friend List

Remember that your diet isn't just what you eat. It's the music you listen to, what you watch on TV, the media you consume, and the people you surround yourself with. Be mindful of what you put into your body and your energy field.

One of the best pieces of advice from successful people is to surround yourself with people who already have what you want. The conversation will be different, better, in those circles.

Your life is the average of the five people you spend the most time with. Notice what the people in your life talk about. Are they talking about groundbreaking ideas, personal development, ways to better humanity and the planet, exciting new opportunities, business and investment ideas, deep conversations about the universe, wisdom teachings, the great mysteries of life and love? Or are they gossiping, indulging in drama, and talking poorly about other people? Are they expanding or constricting your point of view?

The people you surround yourself with greatly influence your success in all seven areas of your life. Seek out positive groups of influences. Join groups of people who are doing and talking about what you want. And it doesn't have to be all mystical and spiritual. If you want to write a book, join a writers' group. If you want to invest in real estate, go to a real estate investment meetup.

Get friends who not only celebrate your successes with you but also challenge you to grow and inspire you to have new ideas. Friends who will call you out on your bullshit because they love you and know you can do better are priceless.

The problem with hanging out with people with lower standards than you is that they will try to pull you back. Not consciously, of course. They likely love you and want you to be happy, but they may also subconsciously be fearful that if you change and grow, they'll lose you. So they'll say things like, "Don't work so hard. Come have a drink tonight," or find ways to undermine what you're doing and working on. Don't lower your standards so that you don't make others feel bad about themselves. Instead, surround yourself with people who have higher standards than you and you can't help but rise to match them. You can certainly rise up and be the one who inspires those around you to achieve greater success, but make sure you also have friends who inspire you too.

One type of person to really watch out for are people who act like friends but are actually envious of you. These people likely don't truly want to see you succeed. You can pick out these sneaky people from the crowd by the way they act and the language they use. If they don't seem excited about positive things that happen to you, if they talk more about themselves and don't seem interested in your life unless something is wrong, if they are often competing against you and use language that makes it obvious they are jealous, then they probably aren't adding much to your life. Friends should lift each other up, not see each other as competition or try to bring each other down.

Negative people who only ever complain and make you feel drained are another group to avoid. Protect your precious energy. Remember, what you focus on is what you will attract. And listening to someone else's constant drama, gossip, and negativity can affect your own energy field and drag you down. That's not to say you can't comfort a friend in need, but pay attention to people's patterns of behavior and speech and make intelligent choices about who is worth your time and attention. Your time, energy, and attention are your currency in this world. Invest them wisely.

4. Move Your Body

Go for a walk in nature, practice yoga, lift weights, dance, swim, practice martial arts, or find some other movement modality every day, even if it's only for fifteen minutes. Even if it's a gentle movement like mindful stretching, Qi gong, Tai Chi, or chair yoga. They even make seated elliptical machines that fit under your desk. Whatever it takes. Exercise boosts your mood, relieves stress, keeps your body strong and flexible, reduces pain, enhances your cognitive abilities, gives you more energy, gives you better sleep, helps keep your muscles and bones healthy… The list goes on and on. There are so many wonderful reasons to move your body every day, and no matter what level of fitness you are at, there is always something you can do to get started.

If you'd like to come practice yoga with me, you can find my classes at Unite By Yoga, the yoga company I own. I teach online classes as well as in person so you can join from anywhere in the world, and I accept sliding scale payments because I think the powerful practice of yoga should be available to everyone, not just an elite group of people. Pricing yoga outside of certain groups of people's reach is missing the essence of what yoga is all about. My classes are for all levels, and everyone is welcome, even if you've never stepped foot on a yoga mat before. We leave ego and judgment out of the yoga space because comparing yourself to others, even comparing yourself to yourself from the last class you took, is not productive. Everyone is on their own path, their own journey. And no two days stepping onto your mat are the same. It's a different version of you every time, like staring into a rushing river and knowing that even though the river is the same, the individual water molecules are always new and different.

Your body is incredible because it tells the story of your life. The activities you did as a child helped shape your bones. What you do for work affects your body, like if you stand a lot or sit a lot. Everything you've been through—things you've had to do, your joys, your triumphs, your traumas, your fears, everything you've risen above—your body holds all of that. Because of that, the top of your femur bone might not fit into your hip socket in the same way that mine does, so for example our lizard poses might look very different. And that's normal and okay and beautiful.

We all wear masks and armor as we move through our life. We have a mask for work, a mask for our family, a mask for our friends, a mask for the grocery store. And armor is great because it protects you and might have kept you safe at one point in your life, but if you never take it off, it gets rusty, stiff, and stuck. And as you move on your mat and get into a flow state and close your eyes, you get to remove bits and pieces of that armor, take off that mask. You can shed labels society might place on top of you or that you might place on top of yourself—a friend, a partner, an employee, a boss, a parent, a child, whatever it is—and instead get back to that core, that center, that stillness within you. Because that's who you really are. That's your *true* nature. You are vast and expansive and magnificent and ancient.

5. Keep Adding to Your Pile of Goodness

Finally, do things that bring you joy. We're here to have experiences as human beings on planet Earth, so go experience it! Being spiritual or successful doesn't mean you have to live in a monastery high in the mountains, practice celibacy, and give up your worldly possessions. It also doesn't mean you have to live in a mega mansion, go on expensive retreats, and be into biohacking and all the latest health apps. If those things appeal to you and make you feel fulfilled, then by all means do them, but you don't need any outside things. Inner peace and self-love come from within. And don't try to be something you're not. Be true to yourself. The world would be missing something without your unique energy.

I know plenty of people who say they're spiritual, are into crystals, post positive quotes on social media, get their tarot cards read, and attend full moon ceremonies who still haven't found inner peace. And I know people who are religious, attend group prayer, dress in a certain way, avoid certain foods, and study their sacred texts who hold such strong judgments of others that it teeters on hatred. And finally I know people who own their own businesses, belong to country clubs, and love fashion who are beacons of kindness, joy, compassion, and generosity.

You don't have to do anything special to be worthy and deserving of love. That is already your birthright simply because of your existence. You can still be a good person if you love to travel the world, go on exotic food tours, dance in clubs, collect fine wines, play video games, invest in the stock market, buy real estate, watch football, or anything else. The question is why do you do those things? Do you do them because they bring you joy? Do you do them out of self-love? Do they bring you a sense of peace and harmony? Or do they stem from fear, bring feelings of guilt or shame, and serve as a way to avoid your feelings?

Being spiritual also doesn't mean you have to be serious all the time. Have fun! Laugh. Enjoy your life. Do things that make you happy and add to your life. Keep adding to your pile of goodness. Do things out of love, things that bring you joy and peace, things that make you feel alive.

I encourage you to commit to the twenty-one days. That amount of time is really just a blink in this experience we call life, and by starting a new set of routines and habits, you will completely disrupt old ones that have kept you stuck. In a matter of weeks, you could be feeling like a completely new you, with more clarity, less stress, and a healthier body and mind. Every day, in every way, you'll notice yourself getting better and feeling better. The perfect time to start becoming the new you is right now.

So now that you have a road map, let's explore overcoming common challenges and the importance of resiliency.

CHAPTER 9

PERSISTENCE, RESILIENCE, AND ADAPTATION

One of my favorite quotes is by Henry David Thoreau. "If one advances confidently in the direction of his dreams, and endeavors to live the life which he has imagined he will meet with a success unexpected in common hours. He will put some things behind; will pass an invisible boundary; new, universal, and more liberal laws will begin to establish themselves around and within him, or the old laws will be expanded, and interpreted in his favor in a more liberal sense and he will live with the license of a higher order of beings."[8] I love this quote because he's talking about if you let go of the common way of thinking that you've been taught, manifest what you want, take steps to get it, and let go of the how, the universe will rearrange everything to deliver your dream life to you.

---

8   Henry David Thoreau, *Walden* (Boston: Ticknor and Fields, 1854)

Sometimes the universe delivers in unexpected ways. It's all about trusting wholeheartedly and having not a single doubt in your mind. It's like a trust fall. Forget about all of your current circumstances that you think might prevent you from getting your thing, no matter how dire they seem. Your current circumstances do not dictate the direction of your life in the future. Your education, your past, your experience level, your current career and friendships and relationships, your health—none of those dictate where you will go in the future.

Don't worry about how it's going to happen. It's not up to you to decide how it happens. It's up to you to decide what you want, to tune yourself into the frequency, to take steps toward the thing you want, and to trust wholeheartedly that it's going to happen for you.

Oftentimes we get the thing we're manifesting in a way we could have never even imagined. Things you thought were impossible become possible. The universe will rearrange everything in your path in order for it to open up before you. Once you make a decision and take action toward the life of your dreams, the universe will move barriers out of your way, the right people will appear in your life to help you, doors that didn't even exist before will appear and unlock, you'll heal what needs to be healed, and circumstances will completely rearrange around you.

The universe is an intelligence that knows how to do and deliver all things in a very simple way. As human beings we tend to overcomplicate things. We think A needs to happen, then B, then C, and so on. We think that we need to make $100,000 this year in order to make $200,000 next year. But the universe has ways of jumping us quickly and easily from A to Z. It's like the child's game Chutes and Ladders. We think that we have to trudge from square to square, when really we can shoot up a ladder.

And the way that the universe puts things into place ends up being for the greatest good of all involved. For example, when I wanted to become director of the yoga company I worked for, I didn't know how it would happen because someone already had that position. But I just trusted wholeheartedly that it would happen and right at the perfect time for me to step into the role, the person who had that job decided to leave the company. This happened with my previous job in the tech industry as well when I moved into the role of head of marketing. I was ready to move up but never imagined a senior-level executive would step away and I was second in command, so it looked like I had hit a ceiling. But that person did end up leaving, and at exactly the right time, to start a new company and become their own CEO. If someone has the position of your dreams at work, then the universe will inspire them to move for another position, company, or even town that better suits their needs for where they are at that particular point in their lives, something that will help them evolve on their own soul journey. And the same is true for every aspect of life. It's a giant puzzle, one that we could never fully conceive of from the vantage point we're at, and it always falls perfectly into place, exactly as it's meant to.

There's no competition with the Law of Attraction. Receiving the thing you want and living in abundance doesn't drain the abundance from anyone else. You getting more does not mean someone else gets less. When you download a song, there's one more copy of it out in the world, not one less. There is enough for everyone to get exactly what they desire to live their dream life and enjoy abundance. When we spread this knowledge so that all people can rise up and enjoy their gifts, we help to bring more light into the world and raise the consciousness of all of humanity. As they say, rising tides lift all ships.

Trust the Process

Let go of trying to control so much or you'll drive yourself crazy. Know that you're on the path you're meant to be on. The journey is as important, if not more important, than the destination. It's during the journey that you learn and grow. Remember we're here to have experiences, learn soul lessons, and practice manipulating energy until we've mastered it. This might be brand new to you, like a baby taking your first steps. Keep putting one foot in front of the other and keep going.

Trusting the process can seem scary or weird or foreign at first. Especially for those of us who like to be in control or have type A personalities or like to have a plan for everything. But the thing is, you're never truly in control. There's only the illusion of control. You came here with a few set plans: how you're going to be born, some big life circumstances that will give you the opportunity to grow, and how you're going to die. Beyond that, you can call into existence in your life that which you desire by shifting your thoughts, but you can never truly control everything. All you can control are your thoughts and the way you respond to things. When you flow with life rather than clenching your jaw and tightening your shoulders against it, the ride is much smoother and more pleasant. So many of us tend to carry so much tension around just because we're trying to control something that we were never meant to control in the first place. So take a deep breath, soften your shoulders away from your ears, unhinge your jaw, relax your throat, unfurrow your brow. And try to soak up and enjoy everything about this wild adventure that we call life.

Know that the old adage "When one door closes another one opens" is so true. Sometimes what feels like an ending is in actuality a beginning. Sometimes the universe will slam a door shut in your face in order to redirect you to where you're meant to be. And sometimes the universe will clear people out from your life who are not meant to go further on the path with you. These things might feel like losses in the moment, but they are all happening *for* you. Remember that it might not happen in the way you think it will. You might think you're coming close because things are starting to align and you might think you see the path ahead only to have the universe redirect you because you're meant to take a sharp right, not go straight, in order to take the fastest route to your dream life. Sometimes doors slam because it's part of your soul lesson too. That you're meant to take a longer route because there is some lesson in there that you need to learn, as part of your agreement for this incarnation. And sometimes it's the universe saving you from something not meant for you. I think about this sometimes when I'm sitting in traffic for instance, that maybe if there had been open roads that day, I would have gotten into a horrific car accident.

Trust that all that is meant for you is already yours and all that you're manifesting is on its way to you. It will effortlessly flow into your life. Instead of worrying about how, instead of stressing out about it, relax and believe that you are deserving and ready to receive. Put yourself in this state completely so that you can match what you want to attract. When you are ready, it will happen.

Never Give Up

One of the best pieces of advice I was taught by my mentors is: *Say yes until you have a good reason to say no*. You never know what seemingly small invitations and opportunities will lead to your next big break. Don't hesitate when you see an opportunity. Don't waste your time wavering back and forth. Be decisive. You never know where an opportunity is going to lead you.

There was a story we used to tell in yoga teacher training of a yoga teacher from New York who was offered a gig teaching yoga at an apartment building, and even though he didn't really want to take it, he knew to say yes until he had a good reason to say no, so he did. A few months into teaching there, a new student came into his class. Afterward, she came up to him and told him she loved the class and loved him as a teacher and that he made her feel so welcome. She told him that the reason she came was because her work was currently looking for a yoga teacher and she offered him a job. It turned out she worked for the United Nations and they were looking for a yoga teacher. So of course he said yes—probably hell yes—and he became the official yoga teacher of the United Nations for many years. And from that, he got countless more opportunities.

I had a similar experience happen with my own yoga company, Unite By Yoga. The local basketball team, who are 7-time NBA champions, reached out asking if we wanted to partner with them and teach yoga to the public at their stadium.

The classes were sponsored by the largest health coverage and care organization in the United States and garnered massive crowds.

Put yourself out there. It can be scary at first, but you need to free yourself from the prison of old, stale, limiting beliefs and step into your power. Summon up all the courage you can muster and take that first step. Then take the next step after that, and the next. Without risk, there is no reward.

The number one reason people don't put themselves out there is because they are afraid of failure, rejection, pain, and other people's opinions. But if we peel that back, it's not failure that they're really afraid of—they're afraid of not being loved. They're afraid that if they fail, people won't love them. Or if they change and strive for greater things, people won't love them. Remember what *A Course in Miracles* says, "Every act is either an expression of love or a call for love." You could say the same for every inaction, too.

I'll let you in on a secret right now: you can't please everyone. Not everyone is going to resonate with you, not everyone is going to love you, not everyone is even going to like you or say nice things about you. But you can't be driven by the what-ifs. I think it's scarier to ask, "What if I don't?" What if you don't step into your power? What if you don't follow your passion? What if you don't stretch beyond your comfort zone? It's far worse to have a list full of regrets at the end of your life because you were scared of what other people might think. Five hundred people will give you five hundred different opinions. Don't let yourself be swayed in five hundred different directions by them.

Follow your heart, it's the only North Star you need.

If someone is attacking your character, insulting you, telling lies about you, criticizing you, or hurting you in some way, it's important to consider the source. Who is this person? Are they someone whose opinion you respect? Are they calm, rational, and level-headed? Or are they someone whose opinion really doesn't matter to you and who is lashing out irrationally and angrily? If you respect their opinion and they are calmly giving you feedback on something that could potentially help you to grow and expand, maybe what they're saying is something to consider. If, however, they are spewing poison at you and trying to make you feel inferior, unworthy, or humiliated it's not worth the time of day to take this personally. Especially if it's coming from someone whose point of view you don't value.

It can be scary to put yourself out there and follow your dreams, and I don't want to lie to you: as you become more and more successful, a lot of times people will try to tear you down. This has nothing to do with you, though. They do it so they can feel more significant about themselves. As they watch you change and flourish, it reminds them that they are not changing and flourishing. And this doesn't even have to be people in your life; it can be people who don't know you, have never met you, have never spoken to you, and don't know anything about you other than what you've shared. We've all seen internet trolls out there attacking strangers. The more successful you get, the more rejection you risk and the more people will judge you, have strong opinions about you, and create stories about you. If someone is attacking your worth and trying to knock you down, they are coming from a place of their own pain and fear. Stand firmly in your confidence, know your worth, trust that what they are saying isn't true, and don't let it affect you.

At the end of the day, you can only be responsible for your own thoughts, beliefs, actions, and reactions to things. You can't change other people, but you can change your own mind. Make the decision to not care about what other people say, do, and think.

All successful people experience fear at one point or another. They're human beings! The difference is that they don't let this fear paralyze them. They summon up courage. "They do it afraid," as Mary Morrissey says. And they don't make decisions from a fearful place. They move through it. Anxiety and excitement are the same emotion—it's all about how you interpret them. You can use that energy to amp you up or to break you down. Even if you try and fail, you'll just learn from it, so why not try? You never know where it might lead. Remember, we're living in a game, a school, a play. All of the things you're afraid of cannot hurt your true self. We're often so caught up in trying to protect ourselves from all of these perceived external threats that we forget they're all part of the illusion. Instead, remember to laugh and have fun. Try to not take it all so seriously.

It's all about staying in a mindset of passion, commitment, and energy and keep visualizing your dream and taking steps toward it. If you don't take steps toward what you're passionate about, that fire you've lit under yourself will eventually fade. Keep riding the high of your excitement, your passion, your purpose, your joy and that momentum will continue to build. As soon as you let in fear and doubt and envy and other low-vibration emotions though, your momentum will come to a screeching halt. Don't give in to those thoughts.

Never give up. Be willing to change your approach if things aren't panning out the way you want. Get creative rather than rigid. And try not to get discouraged. There's always something else you can do. If you think you're at a dead end or a roadblock, you're only looking at it from one angle. Try to take the most objective viewpoint you can. Leave out emotion and all of the lenses you carry around and just look at the thing as a thing. Then look at your Manifest Memoir again and write out another step you could take in the direction of your dream right now and then do it. Write out ten steps you could take and do them all. Something will shake loose. If you go at something with persistence, completely absorb yourself in it, become obsessed with it, journal about it and visualize it, take steps to move toward it, refuse to take no for an answer, then you *will* get that thing. It's not even a question. That is how the universe we live in operates.

Don't just do the same thing over and over again expecting different results. Switch up your approach and try something new. Eventually something is going to work. Somewhere out there in the quantum realm of possibilities is the thing you can try that is going to make it all click and fall into place. Never say to yourself, "I've tried everything," because if you had tried everything, you would have found one path that worked.

We need to retrain ourselves to think from the solution instead of the problem. To think from the result of what you want to achieve, rather than your current circumstances. Think from your dream life, not your current life. Thinking from the problem means that the solution is always floating "out there" somewhere in the future, like a goal that you're constantly striving for but never reach. But when you think from the solution, you're already placing yourself in the awareness and mindset of it. When you flip the script like this, you can see things that you couldn't have seen otherwise.

Be resilient. Grow a thick skin toward the world and your own ego. Be mindful of whom you share your dream with. There are plenty of people out there who are dream crushers. These might be people who love you and don't want to see you hurt if you fail. Having someone else tell you that what you want is impossible is such a downer feeling. But even if they do, don't listen to them. A qualified coach or mentor is the perfect person to offer you encouragement and support. Keep your dreams private from the public and then move silently toward them.

When adversity comes your way, use it to launch you into even more growth. Use it as fuel to become even more steadfast and determined. See it as a gift, as stepping-stones toward your soul's evolution and as a way to grow and awaken even more. When challenges come, you have two choices. You can either become more awakened or go deeper into illusion.

Failure is simply feedback on one way that didn't work. Fail forward. Learn from every mistake you make. Because everyone makes mistakes. Find the lesson, the opportunity, and use it as a launchpad to grow. "Bad" stuff happens to everyone, but inside every adversity there is opportunity. See the lesson and the opportunity in everything.

Thomas Edison tried to create the lightbulb ten thousand times before he achieved it. Ten thousand times! When asked how he kept going after failing so many times, he said, "I didn't fail. I've just found 10,000 ways to not make a lightbulb." It's all about mindset.

With resilience and persistence anything can be achieved.

Watch Your Language

Remember how we talked about the importance of the language you use when you journal? Even while you're speaking in conversation to others, mind your language. Don't say things like "I'm overwhelmed." Flip it into "Up until this moment, I've felt overwhelmed," to avoid claiming the feeling of overwhelm in the present moment. Acknowledge it as something that happened in the past, because by putting it in the past, you're saying that now it has the potential to shift, and the universe hears that. You're giving the universe permission to act on your behalf.

Don't say you have a "problem" or a "challenge" either. Instead, try using the word "opportunity" or "possibility." Try asking yourself what good could be coming from an adversity you are going through or have recently gone through and try journaling about it. If nothing comes to you, try sitting in meditation and asking your Higher Self, or get a QHHT session, or book a session with your mentor or coach and use them as a sounding board. Chances are there's a part of you that already knows the answer. Be open to the messages you receive.

I want to be clear that this is not spiritual bypassing. Don't deny or ignore the fact that you're going through something or something happened to you. Just don't be held back by whatever that thing is. Come from a place of the solution rather than the condition or problem. When you work backward like this, more pathways illuminate before you.

Finally don't ever say that you are triggered. When you say that you're triggered, not only are you playing the victim and playing small, but you're also giving your power away. If you constantly blame other people and outside events for your suffering, you are never going to change the circumstances of your life. When you put out into the universe that you're triggered, you are going to get more situations sent to you that make you feel victimized and triggered. Instead, make a different choice. View your triggers as teachers. Rather than lashing out at the outside world for triggering you, start to work on healing the part of you that was triggered in the first place. By claiming that you're triggered, what you really want is the outside world to change and accommodate your feelings, but you can't control the outside world. The only thing you can control is yourself. And if you tell people that they're triggering you in a combative way, you're just going to cause a defensive reaction and you're not going to get what you wanted in the first place. The way you change the outside world isn't by force, it's by first changing yourself. Step into your power, do the inner work, and heal and then you will see that change reflected in the environment around you.

If you're in the middle of a proverbial storm, Julia Cannon and Kaya Wittenburg offer some great advice. They say to put your consciousness on the other side of it. Imagine yourself on the other side of the giant storm cloud. How would you feel? What would it feel like to look back on everything you had just gone through? What would you want to tell the version of you who is still stuck inside of the cloud? This change in perspective can help shift your mindset. Remember time isn't linear. It's a man-made construct, a rule of our earthly school. In truth, all timelines are happening simultaneously. This is an extremely difficult concept to grasp from our 3D way of thinking, but even if you can't wrap your head around it, maybe you can at least take comfort in knowing there is a version of you who is already through the storm.

Dark Nights of the Soul

We all go through a Dark Night of the Soul. This is a crisis of some sort that wavers your faith, makes you question your beliefs, uproots your life, and shakes the foundation beneath your feet. It's a period of spiritual and personal desolation, a state of feeling deserted or ruined. It often feels like the world is ending, the walls are closing in, everything you know has fallen apart, and your support system seems to have vanished. We are often inconsolable during this time. It could be the death of a loved one, the ending of a marriage, the diagnosis of a life-threatening disease, or any other big event that completely rocks your world and sense of self.

A Dark Night of the Soul is one of the biggest learning moments in our lives and can propel us into spiritual growth if we allow it to. It can be a fast track in personal development where you transition into deeper clarity, spiritual maturity, and understanding of life and your place in the universe. You often end up shedding many conclusions you drew about who you are and what life is, such as your identity, career, relationships, belief system—things that previously helped you construct meaning in your life. You typically never come out of a Dark Night of the Soul the same person as you went in.

I've gone through two Dark Nights of the Soul in my adult life. The most recent one happened when members of a community that I was a part of started spreading lies about me on social media.

The people who posted about me created an invisible filter that distorted everything I had said and done and then flipped it to fit the narrative they were telling. Friends who knew what those people were saying was untrue did not stand up for me. Other people who had told me how much I had changed their life, and how grateful they were for me just months earlier, were now liking posts that were libeling me. Essentially, they were rewriting their experience. It was the strangest thing I had ever watched unfold, like witnessing a live psychology experiment.

The whole experience was traumatic. I felt publicly humiliated and attacked, yet silenced since comments were disabled so I couldn't defend myself. People who had never met me before were helping spread lies about me. It was infuriating and frustrating. I felt unsafe. I feared for my safety and for my family's safety. For a while, the whole experience robbed me of my joy, stripped me of my confidence, and destroyed my trust in people. I was angry, traumatized, and didn't know whom to trust. I just wanted to get away from everyone. My adrenals were in fatigue from all of the stress, which sent me into a Hashimoto's flare-up, and I started rapidly gaining weight. I was in a dark place.

As I sorted through my strong feelings, I realized that the people who had written these hurtful things had made assumptions about me based on the limited amount of knowledge they had. They filled in the knowledge gaps by creating stories in their heads, which they let fester until they built up, and then they posted lies on the internet. *The Four Agreements* teaches us to never make assumptions for exactly this reason: we make up stories in our head that become so distorted and far from the truth and end up causing us distress.

Another one of *The Four Agreements* is to be impeccable with your word. Don Miguel Ruiz explains how unfortunately, in our modern society, most people use the word to spread their personal poison of anger, jealousy, resentment, and hate. Rather than using the word for good, most people use the word to curse and blame others, to find guilt and plan revenge, and to create chaos and destruction. He asks readers to think back on a time when they were angry at someone and wanted revenge, then explains that in order to achieve revenge, they said something to or about another person with the sole intention of causing them harm. People are so calculated in their attempts to bring other people down and then lie to themselves to justify their own actions and feel better about the pain they have caused. They tell themselves that the person deserved their poison and received the proper punishment for their wrongdoing. But of course, this is not true.

I talked to three separate therapists in the months after. I went into the therapy sessions with my tail tucked under and ashamed, explained the whole situation, the nature of the attacks, what was said, admitted I was the person being burned at the stake, was brutally honest about it all. I tried to deliver the events as they happened, without a filter or lens, so that I could get the best advice possible. I expected to be shamed by the therapists like I had by all these people, but it couldn't have been farther from the truth.

All three therapists said it was about boundaries. This was a lesson in having my boundaries up now. The people who had lashed out and attacked me online hadn't set proper boundaries for themselves when they were part of the community, meaning if they didn't like something, they could have made the choice to walk away and leave, to pursue what would make them happy. No one was forced to stay.

The therapists said my work right now was to understand what part of the whole thing belonged to me and what part belonged to other people. The part that belonged to other people, they said, was that they decided to make assumptions and then tell lies based on those assumptions, to place meaning on top of things I might have said or done, to take things personally or to be offended, to see things through their lens only, to anonymously lash out online rather than have a face-to-face conversation, and to rewrite their experience. I hadn't done anything wrong, the therapists assured me. It was the other peoples' interpretation of events and how they'd acted that was the problem and showed where they still had a lot of healing and spiritual growth to do. *We don't see things as they are, we see them as we are.* Just like how we manifest our world, our reality is seen through our own lens and our own story.

The part that did belong to me, according to the therapists, was how I reacted or responded now. Where I went from here. I needed to stop beating myself up about it. They said people's behavior is more about who they are than who I am. They said this event challenged my capacity to not take things personally. You are not responsible for anyone's distorted perception of you, they told me. I needed to stand unyielding in my truth, that I know who I was for these people and how I showed up for them and that my intentions were pure. How they interpreted that was out of my control and not mine to focus on.

I started to pull myself out of the rut. I dove back into the teachings and rituals and self-care habits that I share in this book. The joy crept back into my life.

In addition to the weight gain being caused by a Hashimoto's flare-up, I realized it was also an unconscious attempt to insulate myself from the attacks. Once I healed emotionally, the weight quickly melted off with no effort on my part.

I came back stronger and wiser and more careful with my boundaries and whom I give my energy and attention to. My capacity to not take things personally has expanded, and I try to check myself anytime I catch myself making my own assumptions. I understand now with much more clarity and certainty that the way others behave toward me has much more to do with who they are and the lens through which they view the world than it does with me.

I've since let go of my anger and hurt and forgiven every single person. Thinking about the events and people who were involved is not something I waste my energy on anymore. It's not about finding out the *why* of something that happened. Why is not a spiritual question and obsessing about the "why" isn't useful. Insight doesn't create transformation. Knowing why something happened doesn't change the trajectory of your future. It's instead about asking *what* and *how* questions like, "*What* next step can I take?" or "*How* can I use this opportunity to grow?"

The only two paths forward are to forgive and get better or to hold onto resentment and get bitter.

Mary Morrissey likes to say she has "two black belts: one in success and one in failure." I am inspired by her story. She built a multimillion-dollar business and lost everything overnight when it came out that her husband at the time embezzled money from their company. The newspapers dragged her name through the mud because people accused her of being involved or knowing about it, but she picked herself up and built another multimillion-dollar business, paid all the money back, and tells her story openly at every event like I've just told you mine.

There is nothing so bad that can happen to you that you don't deserve to build your dream life. And no matter how leveled you feel, you can always build up. You can always start over. All you can do in the moment is try to make it right the best you can, and then move forward with your life, taking the lessons with you, and letting go of the emotions. Always do the best you can, don't take anything personally, don't make assumptions, and be impeccable with your own word even when people are throwing daggers of lies at you. And forgive everyone involved, including yourself. No one deserves to be punished forever.

Now that I'm on the other side and have enough distance from it all, I can actually say that I'm grateful it all happened. I really mean that. My growth accelerated in ways it wouldn't have otherwise and I learned things and made realizations that I couldn't have possibly imagined before. It's the difference between sitting in on a lecture and participating in a lab where you get to be hands on. And the best part? I love this version of who I have become!

Looking back at the events, I see so clearly that, though all those people likely believed they were doing the right thing, by taking the route of attacking, they became the very thing they were fighting against. We go back to the old adage that "hurt people hurt people." And so the cycle continues.

Until someone decides to break it.

Since our lives are so intertwined and we live in such an interconnected world, all it takes is one person to summon up the courage to make a different choice. One person to be able to watch the evening news and choose to not feel passionate anger or the need for vengeance when they hear about people who have caused others harm. One person to not lash out emotionally when they have been let down and their trust is betrayed. One person to not feel blind rage and instead choose to let it go when they are being insulted. One person to choose kindness even when they are being attacked. One person to respond to hate with love. As this one person makes the choice to respond in a new way to an old paradigm, they make the path easier for everyone else. As more people follow suit, eventually a tipping point will be reached in the cosmic canvas and all of humanity can boldly step closer toward love and peace.

Things happen in life that test you, and it's how you manage those things that dictates the outcome you're going to have. And it's how you come out on the other side, whom you *choose to be* on the other side, that really matters. It's digging in and staying true to your principals even when it feels like the world is against you. Every tragedy, every heartbreak in life, contains within it a hidden Easter egg, and once you discover it, tremendous healing, growth, and leveling up takes place.

You'll always have haters, you'll always have critics. There may even be people out there who are determined to bring you down.

Remember, this says much more about who they are as people than who you are. Don't take things personally. Stay on your own course. We all have the same amount of time in a day, a month, a year. How you choose to spend your time and energy matters.

We all go through at least one Dark Night of the Soul in our life, and it often hits like a battering ram when we least expect it. But it doesn't come until you have accumulated up until that time all you need to not only survive it but to heal, grow, and then thrive from the experience. Let your Dark Night of the Soul be the rocket fuel that launches you forward.

CHAPTER 10

WHAT IF NOTHING CHANGES?

So let's say you've dived headfirst into all of the teachings and exercises that I've laid out, but every single thing in your Manifest Memoir hasn't come to fruition yet. Now what?

Keep going. Don't stop. The first twenty-one days were to help you form good habits and release the ones that are no longer serving you, but this is a lifelong endeavor. Remember, we're here to learn how to do this. These things take practice. Keep refining your vision. Keep adding details. Keep taking steps toward your dream life. Some people take many lifetimes to even awaken to the possibility that they have this power while others master it in a single one. There is no set time line for you. This is not a race. You can have as many tries as you need to pass this "level." You are perfect exactly as you are, and you are enough, and the pace you are moving at is exactly the pace you should be moving at. You are a spiritual being here to have experiences and learn these lessons and then once you do, you'll be off to the next school. An infinite number of souls are ahead of you on this path and an infinite number of souls are behind you on this path. It's a continuously flowing cycle back to and from Source.

Check your thoughts. Doubt cancels out. You might be doing all of the exercises to a T, but then over drinks on a Friday night, you complain to a friend about how it never happens for you. If you've got energy and momentum moving in one direction and then create energy and momentum in the opposite direction, then all that's going to happen is…nothing.

I had a client, Abby, who was trying to manifest a romantic relationship into her life. She was in her early forties and felt like she was running out of time. Abby was a petite woman, very fit from all of the CrossFit she liked to do, and had brown hair, freckles, and an infectious smile. She had a lively social life filled with lots of close friends and was excelling in her career. She was rich in every area of her life except for her romantic relationships.

She had practiced the Law of Attraction for quite some time before she came to see me, and it had worked for her for small things. It started with wedding dresses. She journaled that she wanted to see a wedding dress and pretty soon she was seeing them everywhere: on billboards, on commercials, on her social media feed, in store windows she walked by, in magazines, on the cover of books, on T-shirts…literally everywhere she looked. Her life became inundated with wedding dresses.

She started to test it out with bigger and bigger things, and it became a fun hobby for her. She even manifested a raise.

As much as this hobby delighted her, Abby had a block when it came to manifesting a meaningful romantic relationship into her life. She had never been in a relationship for longer than a few months, and all she wanted was to find a good man to marry, one who shared her love of fitness and could be her workout buddy, and to start a family with. A family was what she wanted more than anything in the world and what she thought about constantly, every day. She journaled on it. She emptied out closet space for her new partner. She was on all of the dating apps and putting herself out there. On paper, she was doing all the right things.

Sometimes she would get close. She would meet a guy she'd had great conversations with and he would sweep her off her feet on the first date. He would show up with flowers, and they would have a great time and laugh and connect and she would leave feeling like she was floating on air. *Maybe this is the one*, she would cautiously think.

And then after they parted ways, her anxiety would bubble up and her thoughts would start spiraling. What if he never calls again? What if he met someone better? What if he just slowly faded out or worse, completely disappeared? What if he thought she wasn't that great? What if he was love-bombing her? And then the exact thing that she feared most would happen. He'd slowly stop responding to her messages before finally telling her he realized he needed to take more time for himself before getting into a relationship. Sometimes she would try to have a conversation with the guy if she felt him pulling away. Sometimes she stepped back herself to play hard to get. Sometimes she would mention her past experiences and how they caused her to feel triggered by the lack of communication. Other times she "played it cool." No matter how she reacted to these men pulling back, the results were always the same. In the end, they would leave. And it happened over and over and over again. And every single time these men would be in a serious relationship with another woman within a matter of months. Every. Single. Time.

"This always happens," she would tell me during our sessions.

"Up until now this used to happen," I would offer in correction.

If nothing is happening for you, remember that it could be as simple as needing to reframe statements to help our mind understand that the condition isn't always or never, and that just because something happened in the past doesn't mean the cycle will always continue. Our past doesn't have to define us.

Through working with me, she learned to shake this doubt in her mind and this negative self-talk. Thinking is just the process of asking yourself questions. If you want better quality results, you need to ask yourself higher quality questions. She started to focus on what she did want rather than what she didn't and recognized her fears when they started spiraling. She was so close on her own since she understood the Law of Attraction so well, and working with me as her coach helped refine her process and calibrate her vision. She ended up meeting someone who made her feel like the most important person in the world soon after we began our work together. They are now happily married with their first child on the way.

Sometimes asking for help from the right people can mean the difference between our dreams coming true or not. There's nothing like support to help you move along. It can often take an objective third party to figure out that you're sabotaging yourself. Or sometimes you're more willing to listen when you're told that by a professional coach rather than by a close friend. After all, it's difficult to hear that the common denominator in a string of failed relationships is you. It takes being willing to do the work and being willing to really examine your wants, thoughts, beliefs, emotions, words, and actions to see if they are aligned. And then to make some hard changes if necessary. This can be challenging to navigate alone.

Telling your dreams to another person helps energize them and put even more momentum behind them. But like I mentioned earlier, be careful about whom in your life you tell them to. Some family members and friends might unintentionally squash your dreams. That's why working with a professional coach can be so empowering. A gifted mentor, like a life coach, can help you go far. A life coach will help you tailor and refine all of the steps here and help you catch yourself where you might be slipping up without even realizing it. They'll help you get your language laser tight. They'll help you build up your dream until it is so real you can see it, taste it, hear it, smell it, and then they'll help you live into it. They'll help you forgive those who need your forgiveness, not for those people but for you, so you can let go of those feelings of hurt, anger, and resentment that energetically block your flow. They'll assist you on your healing journey. They'll help you release repressed emotions and fear and build up your resiliency and self-confidence. They'll help you change your mind.

I've helped my clients on their journey to living a life they find fulfilling, meaningful, and joyful, a life they would rate ten out of ten in all seven areas. And I'd love to help you too. I offer multiple ways to work with me. Through my various coaching programs, I help you get clear on your vision and guide and support you so that you can step inside the life of your dreams.

Think of it as a way to level up from the material you've just learned in this book and vibrate even higher so that you may attain all that you desire with even more speed and consistency. You can even come practice yoga with me online if you'd like! Visit my website to get started today. I would be so honored to help you accelerate into the life of your dreams.

Only Gratitude Remains

We've been on quite a journey together. You've come so far as you've turned the pages of this book, and I encourage you to take a moment to reflect on all that you've learned, absorbed, put into practice, and accomplished.

You've learned that, simply by changing your mind about something, it can completely alter the way you see the world and how you move through it. You've been introduced to new ways in which to view reality and life and have opened a piece of your mind in the process. You've learned how to deal with fear when it arises and how to shut out your ego when it tries to instill doubt in you. You've learned how to use your thoughts as tools to help you understand what is missing in your life and what you want to add in. You've replaced the mindless stream of subconscious thoughts with positive mantras, so that even when you're not consciously paying attention, you're vibrating at a higher frequency. You learned a method for journaling and ways to also include your environment into the mix to help you manifest all that you desire. You've taken stock of what you would truly love to have in your life and written out a detailed Manifest Memoir that you now read every night. And you've listed out action steps—and then acted on those steps!—for each part of that dream life. You've forgiven others and yourself, so that your mind and heart are clear and you are no longer holding on to negative emotions about the past. And you've rewired your brain when it comes to how you understand illness, so that all of the healing modalities you've begun to incorporate into your routine can have an even greater effect. You've prioritized self-care to calm your nervous system and soothe your stress response. You've learned to not take things personally and to not make assumptions. And you've learned how to be resilient and adapt and be relentlessly persistent in marching onward toward your goals.

You've heard some stories along the way, some in which you might see yourself, and seen how myself and others have utilized these techniques to achieve the greatest good in our lives. And I've let you know how you can work with me moving forward if you'd like to.

What we've really done together is shaken off the dust of our pasts and reinvented ourselves into more empowered, stronger, more joyful, lighter versions of ourselves, so that we can live with more love, more happiness, more peace, and be the best versions of ourselves for those whose lives we touch. We've gotten a little closer to completing our lessons here together on this earthly plane.

You are a powerful spiritual being. You are bigger than any failure, than any rejection, than your past, than anything anyone can throw at you. You are a spiritual being having a human experience. You are in a game, a play, a school. And you are the lead player, actor, and student. You get to make this life of yours exactly what you want it to be. Nothing can hold you back.

You have nothing to be afraid of. Recognize that you are a vast, expansive light of pure energy and love. A piece of Source.

And we are all connected in a deep, ancient, sacred place that resides within each of us. We are all reflections of each other.

You were put here on this planet to have experiences, so go out and have as many as you possibly can. You were put here to learn and grow and expand, so keep seeking knowledge. If something in this book lit a spark in you, I encourage you to follow that thread and read more about that topic. Keep using the exercises that have resonated with you. The more you do them, the more powerful of a cumulative effect they will have. Read your Manifest Memoir every night, keep forgiving others and yourself, keep releasing repressed emotions and feel the new ones, keep taking steps in the direction of your d7ream life. You have made such amazing progress so far as you've worked through the very real task of shedding things that no longer serve you and reclaiming your life. Be proud of yourself. And don't hide in the shadows. Please, share your light. Share your gifts with the world.

So I encourage you now to go confidently into the world. Touch people's lives. Spread joy. Practice patience. Teach forgiveness. Be compassionate. See things from other points of view. Bathe in the ecstasy of living a full life. And bring into your life all that you would love to have.

And if you need assistance, I'm here to be a beacon to help you navigate.

I can't wait to see what you accomplish and what gifts you bring to humanity.

With immense gratitude for you, my soul family,

Kris Ashley

LEARN MORE

This book wouldn't be what it is without these very special teachers who lit the pathway before me. I encourage you to look each of them up. They expand on their respective topics much more than I have and they have vast amounts of knowledge that they readily share. I am eternally grateful to them all.

These books by these incredible authors, whose work and teachings inspired so much of this book:

Alan Cohen, *A Course in Miracles Made Easy: Mastering the Journey from Fear to Love* (Mill Valley, CA: Foundation for Inner Peace, 1976)

A Course in Miracles (Workbook for Students section) by the Foundation for Inner Peace, available at: https://acim.org/acim/en

Anita Moorjani, *Dying to Be Me: My Journey from Cancer, to Near Death, to True Healing* (Carlsbad: Hay House Publishing, 2012)

Bruce H. Lipton PhD, *The Biology of Belief: Unleashing the Power of Consciousness, Matter, and Miracles* (Carlsbad: Hay House Publishing, 2016)

David R. Hawkins MD PhD, *Letting Go: The Pathway of Surrender* (Hay House Inc, First Edition, January 15, 2014)

Dolores Cannon, *Between Death and Life: Conversations with a Spirit* (Huntsville, AR: Ozark Mountain Publishers, 1993)

Don Miguel Ruiz, *The Four Agreements: A Personal Guide to Practical Freedom* (San Rafael, CA: Amber-Allen Publishing, 1997)

Drunvalo Melchizedek, *The Ancient Secret of the Flower of Life*, 2 vols. (Flagstaff, AZ: Light Technology Publishing, 1998)

Gregg Braden, *The Divine Matrix: Bridging Time, Space, Miracles, and Belief* (Hay House Inc, 1st edition, January 2, 2008)

Jóse Silva and Robert B. Stone, *You the Healer: The World-Famous Silva Method on How to Heal Yourself and Others* (HJ Kramer, Reissue edition, December 28, 1992)

Rhonda Byrne, *The Secret* (Atria Books/Beyond Words, 10th Anniversary edition, November 1, 2006)

The teachings of the following individuals:

Julia Cannon and Kaya Wittenburg, whose Facebook Live Webinars on the Dolores Cannon page are always such an inspiration: https://www.facebook.com/DoloresCannonOfficial

Mary Morrissey, whose life coach training program I am so grateful to have been gifted: https://www.bravethinkinginstitute. com/

Tony Robbins, *Unleash the Power Within* (Simon & Schuster Audio, 2020)

These Authors Who Taught Me So Much About Functional Medicine, Health, and Diet:

Amy Myers MD, *The Thyroid Connection: Why You Feel Tired, Brain-Fogged, and Overweight – and How to Get Your Life Back* (Little, Brown Spark; March 16, 2021)

Datis Kharrazian PhD, DHSc, DC, MS, MMSc, FACN, *Why Do I Still Have Thyroid Symptoms? when My Lab Tests Are Normal: a Revolutionary Breakthrough in Understanding Hashimoto's Disease and Hypothyroidism* (Elephant Press, February 2, 2010)

Dave Asprey, *The Bulletproof Diet: Lose up to a Pound a Day, Reclaim Energy and Focus, Upgrade Your Life* (Rodale Books, December 2, 2014)

Izabella Wentz, PharmD, FASCP, *Hashimoto's Protocol: A 90-Day Plan for Reversing Thyroid Symptoms and Getting Your Life Back* (HarperOne, March 28, 2017)

John E Sarno MD, *The Mindbody Prescription: Healing the Body, Healing the Pain* (Warner Books, Inc., October 1, 1999)

And my dear friends who are out there doing their work and making the world a better place:

Subhan Schenker and Shanti Schenker-Skye who run The World of Meditation: An Osho Meditation School at https://worldofmeditation.com/wp/

Dr. Taylor Krick, DC at https://www.washwellnesscenter.com/ and The Autoimmune Doc Podcast with Dr. Taylor Krick https://podcasts.apple.com/us/podcast/the-autoimmune-doc-podcast-w-dr-taylor-krick/id1562522498

ADDITIONAL REFERENCES

Alan Cohen, "Dealing with Difficult People" as heard at: https://www.youtube.com/watch?v=KlW6dsvWtsg

Bessel A. van der Kolk, *The Body Keeps the Score: Brain, Mind, and Body in the Healing of Trauma* (Penguin Audio, February 16, 2021)

Bruce H. Lipton PhD, "The Nature Of Dis-Ease," (February 8, 2012) Retrieved from: https://www.brucelipton.com/the-nature-dis-ease/

Dr Bruce Lipton, "Placebo Effect VS No-Cebo Effect" as heard at: https://www.youtube.com/watch?v=-jw00Pux5Fs&t=35s

Ellen J. Langer, *Counterclockwise: Mindful Health and the Power of Possibility* (New York, NY: Ballantine Books, 2009)

Gregg Braden, *The Isaiah Effect: Decoding the Lost Science of Prayer and Prophecy* (New York: Three Rivers Press, 2001)

Irving Kirsch PhD, *The Emperor's New Drugs: Exploding the Antidepressant Myth* (Basic Books, Reprint edition, March 8, 2011)

J. Bruce Moseley, Kimberly O'Malley, Nancy J. Petersen, et al, "A Controlled Trial of Arthroscopic Surgery for Osteoarthritis of the Knee," *N Engl J Med*, 347 (Jul 11, 2002): 81-88

Julia Cannon, *Soul Speak: Discover the Secret Language of Your Body* (Ozark Mountain Publishing, January 30, 2013)

Ken Keyes, Jr., *The Hundredth Monkey* (Vision Books, 2nd edition, June 1, 1984)

The Many-Worlds Interpretation of Quantum Mechanics, ed. Bryce S. Dewitt and Neill Graham, Princeton Series in Physics (Princeton, NJ: Princeton University Press, 1973)

Sean Carroll, *Something Deeply Hidden: Quantum Worlds and the Emergence of Spacetime* (Dutton, Illustrated edition, September 10, 2019)

William Davis, *Wheat Belly (Revised and Expanded Edition): Lose the Wheat, Lose the Weight, and Find Your Path Back to Health* (Rodale Books, Expanded edition, December 10, 2019)

https://academic.oup.com/ajcn/article-abstract/26/11/1180/4732762

https://www.cnet.com/health/nutrition/sugar-can-lower-your-immune-system/

https://www.curablehealth.com/

https://drwillcole.com/functional-medicine/the-effects-of-gluten-and-going-gluten-free

https://www.scirp.org/pdf/OJI20110200003_20641104.pdf

https://www.youtube.com/channel/
UCSAKgeiblE8CFUVrmd58dWw/videos

https://www.youtube.com/c/
DoloresCannonPastLifeRegression

https://www.youtube.com/watch?v=IIN8r9rgtUM&t=1s

ACKNOWLEDGMENTS

Above all I want to acknowledge Shane, my husband, best friend, and life partner. I feel such deep gratitude to spend my life with someone who believes in me so much and who is so inspirational to me. I am in constant awe of your persistence, your kindness, your empathy, your capacity to let go, your drive, your communication skills, and your unconditional love. You truly walk the path, and I learn from you every day. Thank you for pushing me when I need it, for always seeing the best in me, for teaching me so much, for encouraging me to strive for more, for learning and growing with me, for listening, for trying all of the things I introduce you to with an open mind, for reminding me of my own beliefs in moments of darkness, for celebrating all of the wins with me, for standing beside me through the losses, for adventuring with me, and for making life so much fun.

And Dad, thank you for always being my biggest cheerleader. For telling me you are proud of me no matter how big or small the achievement. For instilling confidence in me to go out and chase my dreams. For your generosity. For paving the way with your own entrepreneurial spirit. For always having my back. For passing onto me your love of animals and plants. For all of the adventures you've taken me on. And for teaching me not to care what anyone else thinks.

And to Soda Pop. You are my spirit animal, the ET to my Eliot, and just love personified in the cutest, fluffiest little body. We've been through so many incarnations together, and I know we'll always be orbiting around each other through lifetimes to come. Thank you for sharing this adventure called life with me, for your sweetness, your silliness, and for teaching me unconditional love every day. I am so thankful for each moment I get to spend with you, as each one is such a gift. I love you so much it hurts my heart.

To my in-laws, Peggy and Paul. You are such beacons of love and kindness and true teachers by example. Thank you for always listening to me, for being so open-minded, and for loving me like your own daughter.

To Ken Dunn at Helping People Press, thank you for taking a chance on me. For your guidance in all things coaching, writing, and digital marketing. For showing me by example what it means to be a good coach for your students.

To Debra L. Hartmann, editor extraordinaire, thank you for being such a joy to cocreate with.

To all of my readers, I've been a teacher in various capacities in my life. I taught English, I teach yoga, I ran yoga teacher trainings where I taught other people how to teach yoga, and I'm a life coach. In all four professions I have found without fail that the way to best learn material is to teach it. When you have to explain its complexities to other people, you absorb information in a whole different way. In much the same way, writing this book has allowed me to glean deeper meanings from the teachers who I hold such reverence for and from my own lived experiences. It was incredibly healing and cathartic to write this book, and I came to understand the lessons in much more profound ways as I explored how best to make them accessible. So thank you, reader, for holding me up and supporting me as I hope reading this book has done for you.

ABOUT THE AUTHOR

Kris Ashley is a life coach, motivational speaker, yoga teacher, and owner of the yoga studio Unite By Yoga. She received both her bachelors and master's degrees in creative writing and is humbled to now be sharing her teachings and stories through the written word. In her free time, Kris can be found reading books, watching documentaries, attending seminars and retreats, and listening to podcasts in order to keep growing as she believes the learning and growth is never over. She also loves spending time out in the sunshine with her family, friends, husband, and dog. She resides in California.

For information on Kris's life coaching, online courses, seminars, and more, visit: www.krisashley.net. To practice yoga with Kris, visit www.unitebyyoga.com/

9 781738 641604